CAMBRIDGE LIBRARY COLLECTION

Books of enduring scholarly value

Archaeology

The discovery of material remains from the recent or the ancient past has always been a source of fascination, but the development of archaeology as an academic discipline which interpreted such finds is relatively recent. It was the work of Winckelmann at Pompeii in the 1760s which first revealed the potential of systematic excavation to scholars and the wider public. Pioneering figures of the nineteenth century such as Schliemann, Layard and Petrie transformed archaeology from a search for ancient artifacts, by means as crude as using gunpowder to break into a tomb, to a science which drew from a wide range of disciplines - ancient languages and literature, geology, chemistry, social history - to increase our understanding of human life and society in the remote past.

A Wandering Scholar in the Levant

The archaeologist D. G. Hogarth (1862–1927) was, when he died, keeper of the Ashmolean Museum and president of the Royal Geographical Society. He was instrumental in launching T. E. Lawrence's career, employing him at Carchemish and encouraging him to learn Arabic. This book, published in 1896 and described by Lawrence as 'one of the best travel books ever written', relates a journey through Ottoman Turkey, with additional chapters on Egypt and Cyprus. It combines a highly readable account of the practicalities and pitfalls of archaeology with Hogarth's (often unsympathetic) opinions on political problems of the area, including the position of the Armenians and Kurds. Hogarth subsequently became acting director of the Arab Bureau in Cairo during the First World War, and attended the Versailles peace conference. This book illuminates the experiences that developed Hogarth's political views and the close relationship between archaeology and politics in the Middle East in the period.

T0370878

Cambridge University Press has long been a pioneer in the reissuing of out-of-print titles from its own backlist, producing digital reprints of books that are still sought after by scholars and students but could not be reprinted economically using traditional technology. The Cambridge Library Collection extends this activity to a wider range of books which are still of importance to researchers and professionals, either for the source material they contain, or as landmarks in the history of their academic discipline.

Drawing from the world-renowned collections in the Cambridge University Library, and guided by the advice of experts in each subject area, Cambridge University Press is using state-of-the-art scanning machines in its own Printing House to capture the content of each book selected for inclusion. The files are processed to give a consistently clear, crisp image, and the books finished to the high quality standard for which the Press is recognised around the world. The latest print-on-demand technology ensures that the books will remain available indefinitely, and that orders for single or multiple copies can quickly be supplied.

The Cambridge Library Collection brings back to life books of enduring scholarly value (including out-of-copyright works originally issued by other publishers) across a wide range of disciplines in the humanities and social sciences and in science and technology.

A Wandering Scholar
in the Levant

D. G. HOGARTH

CAMBRIDGE
UNIVERSITY PRESS

CAMBRIDGE UNIVERSITY PRESS

Cambridge, New York, Melbourne, Madrid, Cape Town,
Singapore, São Paolo, Delhi, Tokyo, Mexico City

Published in the United States of America by Cambridge University Press, New York

www.cambridge.org
Information on this title: www.cambridge.org/9781108041911

© in this compilation Cambridge University Press 2012

This edition first published 1896
This digitally printed version 2012

ISBN 978-1-108-04191-1 Paperback

A

WANDERING SCHOLAR

IN THE LEVANT

Photo by J. A. R. Munro.

Frontispiece.   See p. 140

VIEW OF GYUKSUN (COCUSUS) IN THE ANTI-TAURUS.

A

WANDERING SCHOLAR

IN THE LEVANT

By DAVID G. HOGARTH

M.A., FELLOW OF MAGDALEN COLLEGE; SOMETIME CRAVEN FELLOW IN THE
UNIVERSITY OF OXFORD; F.S.A.

WITH ILLUSTRATIONS

LONDON
JOHN MURRAY, ALBEMARLE STREET
1896

LONDON :
SRADBURY, AGNEW, & CO. LD., PRINTERS, WHITEFRIARS.

CONTENTS.

CHAPTER I.

THE SCHOLAR'S CALLING.

CHAPTER II.

TRIALS OF A SCHOLAR.

CHAPTER III.

THE ANATOLIAN.

CHAPTER IV.

THE GREAT RIVER EUPHRATES.

CHAPTER V.

AN IMPRESSION OF EGYPT.

LIST OF ILLUSTRATIONS.

A

WANDERING SCHOLAR

IN THE LEVANT.

CHAPTER I.

THE SCHOLAR'S CALLING.

Antiquitas saeculi juventus mundi—Early wanderers—
The Scholar as explorer—Cities of the dead—Inscription hunting—The peasant's mind—Hittite stone
at Bor—A night adventure—Romance and reality—
Antica buying—Difficulties of dealing—The peasant
scores.

To be at once a Scholar and a Wanderer
is to indulge the least congruous desires.
In the same hour you will gratify the last
refinement of intellectual curiosity and obey
a call from the first rude state of nature.
For the "wandering fever" is in a sense a
temptation of original sin, still heard across
the ages, and the scholar finds a subtle joy

B

in the returning to the wilderness rather in spite than because of his being a scholar.

And therein lies a danger to him in so far as he pursues a profession. For his is really a calling like any other, to be pursued professionally ; he is an agent of science, a collector of raw material for the studies of other men. But the life of the Wanderer, himself a law to himself, conduces to a certain Bohemian habit of mind, apt, when concerned with antiquity, to issue in the easy specialism of the *dilettante* or to fall to the idle wonder of the sightseer ; and in either case the scholar may become that most profitless of amateurs, a picker and chooser among the quaint and curious things that have drifted down to us on the stream of time.

In either case let him recall a famous aphorism of Bacon — *antiquitas saeculi juventus mundi*—and apply it thus. The relics of ancient days are all that remain to us of the conditioning circumstance of the young world's life ; they pertain not to an epoch of mysterious greatness or of "giants that were in those days," but to the infinitely little in which our auto-biography begins, and are not to be looked at with wide-eyed wonder by the modern, who is himself the roof and crown of things. The reverence due to antiquity is that paid by an adult to a child ; and whenever we think of the ancient world as aged, we are unconsciously under the spell of an ambiguity of our language which admits as a synonym for both epi-thets the same word "old." It is true that in certain fields of achievement—in the do-main of the imitative arts, for instance—the young world attained to excellence not since surpassed ; but if the whole circumstance of life be taken into account, the Hellene, with his conception of a flat world and a geocentric universe, stands as much below ourselves as the boy, apt in physical ath letics, stands below the adult who no longer may be able either to leap or to run.

So regarded, the flotsam of antiquity has a function greater and more compre-hensive than to gratify an æsthetic sense or stimulate imagination; the Scholar, seeking diligently and with pain for every trifling remnant, is justified of his labour, and the world, too, is justified which sends him out again and sets a value on his research. After all, in how few do ancient monuments really gratify an æsthetic sense, or stimulate imagination! How many, that see it, are convinced by the Parthenon? and who has not had some dismal hour of disillusion when, all things conducing thereto, he felt nevertheless no mysterious thrill? In the Dionysiac Theatre, looking over that storied balustrade to the blue Saronic sea— what a moment for a Scholar! Sit down on a marble bench, and, shutting out the external world, open your inward eyes on the scene at the Dionysia—tier on tier of happy Athenians, an orchestra gay with grotesque batrachians, and Charon coaching Dionysus in a boat on the stage. Do you catch the rustle of the long-robed audience and their quick response to Aristophanes? No, emphatically no, you do not! you are conscious only of the sun on your back and commingling scents in your nose; faint and far come street cries and the raucous echo of a Teutonic voice on the Acropolis above. Imagination has condemned you to a downright dismal failure, and Candour calls you to get up and go away.

This Trade of the Wandering Scholar is a thing of yesterday. Islam was long all powerful to exclude from the Levant, and European discovery followed the sun till it had completed the circle of the world. The rediscovery of the nearer east was due to Louis XIV. Before his time the dark continent of hither Asia had been penetrated only by a handful of pilgrims, political envoys and adventurers, who observed little and recorded less: such for example as Bertrandon de la Brocquière, who on his way back from Palestine in 1433 limited his interest to the court ceremonial of the Grand Karaman; or the English sailor, Newbery, noting in 1578 only the price of "grograms" in the markets between Erzerum and Brusa ; or Tavernier, who excludes from his itineraries, together with dates and distances, all observations of any human interest whatever. Moslems, Ibn Batuta and Evliya Effendi, lift the curtain where a holy place of Islam had succeeded to a shrine of the Infidel ; but only one Christian, Busbequius, who copied a few lines of the great Ancyran inscription on his way to Amasia, enlightened the ignorance of the West on the ancient wonders of the East. It was the gem-collectors of the *Grand Monarque*, Spon, Tournefort, Paul Lucas and Otter, commissioned to bring back curiosities of antiquity or gobbets of information, who were the real pioneers ; they broke the way for Pococke and Chandler and Leake and Texier, for polite societies, like the English *Dilettanti*, and for governments like the Napoleonic, conducted in the grand style, under whose patronage archæological wandering has become now a professional calling.

As a calling, it demands in practice

much more than a knowledge of antiquities and the methods of recording them. If the Scholar wanders into inland Asia he is fain to play the explorer first and the scholar second ; for the Ottoman Empire has been shut against the West so long and so closely that in many parts he will find himself a pioneer breaking new ground for every science. With so many stepping stones to set in the stream of ignorance, the Scholar had best take not too professional a view of his ostensible calling : maps and political reports, customs and types and folk-lore, eggs and bulbs and butterflies and rocks—all these fill his day with amateur occupations for which his professional interest is probably not the worse ; for after all, he is but practising catholicity, and catholicity will serve him even within the limits of Archæology. The " Remains of Distant Times " are various enough, and the Wandering Scholar may neglect a coin as little as a city.

A city ! That red-letter day which Hamilton marked when he found Isaura, crumbling on its lonely mountain, has come once at least to most explorers of Anatolia—a day on which one breaks into some hidden hollow of the hills and sees grey among the lentisks the stones of a dead town. Such fairy-cities are the name-less pirate-towns that were built on the Cilician slopes in the first two centuries before the Christian era. Water, no longer guided by man through long ducts, has failed on the high lands, and the region remains as it was left a thousand years ago, a vast Pompeii, where no man has rebuilt or destroyed. In its capital, Olba, citadel, walls, streets and roads are choked with brush-wood. A triple arch leads into the Forum; on the left the façade of a Temple of Fortune stands in the brake, and in front rise the fluted columns of the Olbian Zeus, whose priests were kings. Passing a ruined portico, the explorer lights suddenly on a theatre lined with tangled vegetation sprouting from every crevice in auditorium and scene. But nothing in the city is more wonderful than the road leading from it

[To face p. 8.

TEMPLE OF ZEUS AT OLBA

to the coast. Mile after mile its embanked pavement runs over the naked
rocks ; mile after mile stones, fallen or
standing, inscribed with the titles of
Roman Emperors, record your progress ;
here you pass a group of tombs, there
clatter through an ancient village, and at
last wind down sweeping curves to the
sea, past towers and tombs rising white out
of the scrub ; and nowhere in the towers or
the villages, on the road or in the city is
there a human thing except the wandering
shepherds.

These dead cities, however, imply to the
Wandering Scholar more than a stimulus
to those "lively and pleasing reflections"
with which Sir John Vanbrugh credited the
"polite part of mankind." Rather they in-
volve long labour with tape-line and camera
in blistering heat, and weary hours of dis-
couragement, spent over inscribed stones
turned upside down, black with exposure
and riddled with worm-holes, such as those
hundred sarcophagi that line the *Sacra
Via* of Hierapolis. Would that arm-chair

critics of published inscriptions had had to read *in situ* certain stones I wot of—to copy, for example, with head down in a square hole of a mosque floor, by the light of a tiny lamp, a stone built into the foundations, while round about hangs a cloud of odorous humanity, hardly bribed to allow this sacrilegious thing to be done at all. You might be less hard in the future, O irresponsible reviewer, on a poor Wanderer who now and again reads Λ for A, or C for O!

The happiest hunting-ground of the exploring Scholar is a graveyard. The peasants love to erect above their dead ancient *stelai* and milestones, partly because they find these shaped ready to their hands, partly because they have a vague belief that the mysterious writing will bring good luck in another life. Where milestones occur in groups of five or six, as in the Anti-Taurus on the great military road to the Euphrates, they are left *in situ*, and by each is laid a Turkman peasant to sleep below the stately record of an Emperor's names and titles.

[To face p. 10.

ROMAN MILESTONES IN THE CEMETERY OF KANLU KAVAK LOOKING TOWARDS THE TAURUS.

Happy the scholar who has only to prowl like a ghoul among such tombstones, for there he is on common ground where an insignificant *bakshish* will induce any Turk or Christian cheerfully to clear a half-buried inscription, however deeply he may have to delve in the resting-place of his nearest relative: but it is another matter altogether when the "written stone" is in a house! The stupidity and cupidity of a man, the fears and malevolence of a woman, baffle him for days, and may condemn finally to failure. The peasant's mind moves very slowly, and he has two processes to accomplish—first, to realise that the stone, which he has seen all his life, is the one which the *giaur* wishes to see; secondly, to convince himself (and his wife or wives) that it is to his interest to show it. There is a little village called Badinlar near the Mæander, first visited in 1884 by Frenchmen, and reported to cotnain no antiquities. Mr. Ramsay followed close on the Frenchmen's heels, and found half-a-dozen "written stones." Three years later he passed again that way with me, and we were rewarded with a series of inscriptions of unique interest relating to a local semi-barbarian worship of Apollo, the remains of whose temple itself we found. It might have been thought that we had exhausted that tiny hamlet, but in 1889 Mr. Ramsay chanced to be there once more and found half-a-dozen stones still uncopied; and I have little doubt that the next scholar who wanders thither will not return empty-handed.

There is but one golden rule in inscription-hunting:—Never believe the inevitable denial : insist, cajole, display coin of the realm till you get one, just one, "written stone :" never mind if you found it yourself, pay somebody all the same. Your hard work is over. After waiting an hour for the first written stone at Comana of Cappadocia in 1891, we were guided to twenty ere the second hour had passed. At Sadagh, the site of Satala, in 1894, a whole day proved blank : on the morrow the peasants were prising up their hearthstones and scrubbing floors and walls that had never been cleaned within living memory, until, in the end, we copied five-and-twenty inscriptions. Rarely, marvellously rarely, the peasant proves exorbitant and obdurate; there is gold in his stone, and he means to have it or an equivalent from you. If you fail to buy, he will hack the inscription to pieces to get at the treasure that he believes to be inside. So there must ensue a contest of wits. A Greek inscription of moderate length you may learn by heart while you haggle—I have never ceased to be half ashamed of having helped to cheat thus a Turk of the Mæander Valley who had coloured purple a valueless *stele* of Motella, and fixed its price at £50—but the owner of a hieroglyphic stone can defy anything but a detective camera, as we found in 1890 at Bor.

Bor is a dirty town, three miles distant from the site of the very ancient and royal city Tyana ; whence had been brought (to be lodged, alas ! in the house of a Greek virago) part of a " Hittite " *stele.* It bore a broken relief of a head, crowned with a kingly tiara, and a long incised inscription in the conventionalised "Hittite" hieroglyphic character, of which, at that time, only one other example was known. Its existence was discovered by Mr. Ramsay in 1882, but the owner would allow no impression to be taken, and frustrated all attempts to make a careful copy. Returning four years later, the discoverer could obtain neither permission to see it, nor even information of its whereabouts. We resolved to make another and last effort in 1890, and took up our quarters in the *khan* at Bor.

The Greek woman had not found a purchaser in ten years, and was not averse now to re-open negotiations. We soon had news of the "black stone," and the same afternoon a guide led us through narrow streets and up a closed courtyard to a barn, where in a dark hole in the mud floor lay the treasure. Deputing a go-between to open negotiations for purchase, we took advantage of the diversion and the owner's apparent graciousness to set to work with pencil and notebook. In a moment the Greek had leapt on to the stone, spreading her petticoats like a hen on a sitting of eggs, while a crowd of friends bustled up to her assistance. Under such circumstances it was impossible to copy an inscription in an unknown character, so we had no resource but to bargain. The Greek demanded 500 liras ; we consulted and made a handsome offer of five for immediate possession. She collapsed in her son's arms, and recognising that the ice was broken, we went away.

All the evening the go-betweens came and went. Next morning our caravan was ordered to start, and the price came down to 40 liras. When the horses were yoked to the baggage-waggon, the market fell to 30: as the waggon rumbled out before us under the *khan* gate, the figure was 25 ; with my foot in the stirrup I was asked for 22, and riding out for 20. Doubtless we could have got the stone for less, but we were pressed for time, and it was worth more than 20 liras. So the bargain was struck and the stone lifted into our waggon. Needless to say, however, we could not hope to carry off so well-known a treasure under the very eyes of the local Governor, unless prepared to pay as much in *bakshish* as in purchase, and, once we had impressions and copies, the stone itself might as well be placed in the Imperial Museum at Stambul. Making, therefore, an ostentatious virtue of necessity, we conveyed it ten miles to Nigdeh, and lodged it there in trust for His Majesty the Sultan. The excitement was immense, and we became the observed of all the town. Strolling that night in the dark over the crowded roof of the *khan*, I heard that certain Franks had tried to escape with a stone worth 10,000 liras, but had been arrested by the police and forced to disgorge! The officials themselves deprecated such wasteful generosity ; and a Government secretary approached us privately next day with a kind suggestion that, if our difficulty related to the conveyance of the stone to

[*To face p.* 16.

THE BOR STONE.

the coast, he could arrange that we should be robbed of it outside the town, and for a slight consideration recover it at the port. Gratefully and regretfully we declined.

The story has a sequel, for the lower half of the same *stele* was above ground. A rumour of it reached us, and a month later I was back in Bor. But the situation had changed : the authorities had made hue and cry for the second stone, and its owner would not reveal his identity unless I pledged myself solemnly to have no dealings with the Government in the matter. I was forced to promise, though I knew that on mountain roads we could not convey secretly anything heavy. When all was dark in the *bazar* a messenger appeared, and my companion and myself crept out of the *khan*. Feeling our way along the walls, we groped through the deep shadow of a labyrinth of unlighted alleys : here we stumbled over a sleeping man, there kicked up a protesting dog, but our European dress passed unnoticed in the dark, and no one followed. We seemed to have been stumbling thus for miles, when the guide halted before a window in a long blank wall. We clambered through and found the scene changed to a luxuriant garden : the hot night air was heavy with the scent of flowering shrubs, through which we brushed to a small plot of grass beside a well, where a courteous Turk was expecting us. Bidding us be seated, he offered grapes and paid the usual compliments, and for nearly half an hour nothing but what was indifferent was said, while we waited, oppressed by the scents and the stillness. At last the host rose silently and, producing a lantern, signed to us to follow to the opposite side of the well. We did so, and there saw shining wet in the small circle of light a black stone. It was indeed the lower half of our *stele*. The figure of a man from the neck downwards, clad in a richly embroidered robe, and shod with upturned shoes, stood out in bold relief ; and at each side of him and below his feet were "Hittite" symbols. The owner hardly allowed a second look before extin-

guishing his lantern. I offered money
for leave to copy the sculpture and inscription, but he would not accept it. I
must take this dangerous thing, which
robbed him of sleep, right away, or he
would sink it again in the well. All means
of persuasion were tried, even to threats
of informing the Government, but these
availed nothing, for he knew that I was
ignorant of his identity, and, as I guessed,
we had not been led to the garden by any
direct road. I could not undertake to
smuggle the stone away : he would listen
to no other suggestion ; and, after long
dispute under the stars, we took leave in
sorrow rather than anger, and dropped
through the window again into the dark
lane.

An epigraphist's experiences are seldom
as like the Arabian Nights as this. Far,
far more often he must tramp about torrid,
odorous villages, beset by an impudent or
hostile crowd, to copy ill-cut, half-erased
epitaphs of no more apparent interest than
modern gravestones. Miserable little Ly-

caonian and Pisidian sites will yield each
a hundred such, mere repetitions of one
formula with varying barbaric names, and
here and there an elegiac tribute of local
manufacture and no conceivable merit.
You must copy against time, for it is nearly
sunset and you are miles from camp; you
are forced to decipher through a field-glass
a stone in such villainous condition that,
unless you could bring your eyes within
an inch or two of the lettering, and with a
knife-blade distinguish chiselling from stone-
flaws, you would distinguish little or nothing
with certainty; you have to read by a
blind man's touch, without his experience,
a text built into the darkest corner of a
windowless room. Worst of all, it is impossible to make the peasants distinguish
between ancient and modern inscriptions,
or between lettering and mouldings or
mere scratches on a rock; all are *yasili*,
" written ;" and accordingly many are the
weary rides up to the hill-tops and down
to the valleys, that result in nothing but
vexation of spirit. An Anatolian, like an

Irish peasant, if kindly disposed, tells you
what you evidently wish to hear : water
a day's march distant is to be found round
the next corner, a plough-marked boulder
is covered with " faces of men and animals
and writing," two ruined huts become a
city.

After a fortnight's inscription-hunting, a
day in a town with the *antica*-dealers is
a solace and a joy ; for even if one knows
but little of coins and gems and seals, the
prizes in the lottery far exceed the blanks,
and each successive bargain reveals new
recesses of the Oriental mind. The most
profitable speculation in Anatolia lies in
the field of bronze city-coinage of Roman
times ; you will buy only pieces in really
fine condition, and may reckon, if you care
to sell again, on making cent. per cent. on
almost all of them. Silver money is a less
certain investment ; prices are proportion-
ately higher, and the types, being more
indestructible, are less rare in Europe.
There is little to fear from forgers in the
interior ; an expert of Tarsus, wise in his

own generation, used to fabricate by the score the common *drachmas* of Alexander the Great to sell to tourists as money used by St. Paul, but evidences of his handiwork have become scarce now, and I think he must have paid his debt to nature or the law. But in the ports—above all in Smyrna —the handiwork of Greek coiners is rife, and one needs be almost as suspicious as in that paradise of counterfeit, the plain of Egyptian Thebes.

Anticas are apt to occur in " pockets." In 1890 we travelled for more than three months, but found not a dozen small objects of any value in all the villages or towns, except in Karaman alone, where every merchant in the *bazar* seemed to have his little hoard of coins ; and there in two hours we bought more than fifty, two unique and very few at all common.   Similarly in 1894 at Aintab there were brought to us from one source or another " Hittite " seals, cylinders, and scarabs of the utmost rarity, together with some thirty of the finest stone implements ; whereas in all our subsequent

S.Systems

Photo by J. A. R. Munro.

[To face p. 22.

Photograph of a Hittite Monument, obtained by inviting local officials
to pose beside it.

journey to the Black Sea we did not find
the tithe of that treasure. It is true that we
had been helped unknowing by unlooked-
for allies—the local police; for long afterwards it leaked out that there had been
driven to us all who possessed antiquities,
for the better testing of a theory that we
were no archæologists but political spies;
and it seems that, after all, the dark suspicion was held to be confirmed by the
fact that we bought only poor, ugly stones
and refused all the gems!

Where one has to deal with ignorant
cunning, all ideals of candour and justice
must be thrown to the winds. If you reside
for months in a certain district you may
offer fair prices only; for, as weeks pass, the
peasants will come to know that you are
a just Englishman, whose habit is not to
bargain. But if the mere wanderer offers
a fair price the odds are great that the
magnitude of it will cause the owner to
conclude at once that the real value of his
antica is enormous; and the caution of the
peasant and the Oriental combined will

bring about the most hopeless disinclination to sell. To combat this mood a European will need all his wits. At Bor in 1890 (after the episode of the stone) I was shown by a Turk a silver seal, supported on three lions' claws, and inscribed with a figure in "Hittite" dress with "Hittite" symbols round him. At a glance I recognised in the seal an absolutely unique thing, to be secured at all costs; but hardly was it in my hand before its owner snatched it away and disappeared. I soon learned that he intended not to sell to me at all; but after some hours he was persuaded to let me have another look at the curiosity, on the express understanding that it was not for sale. A crowd collected, and I remarked that the *antica* was worth two dollars. The instinct of bargain made the bystanders shout at once, "Give half a lira!" I hesitated. "One lira!" "A lira and a half!" "Two liras!" they clamoured rapturously. I made a fatuous stand at that figure. Delighted to have "rushed" me to near six times my price

they turned on the owner of the seal.
"Give it him! Give it him! Two liras!
He said two dollars!" He parleyed a
moment, was lost, and the only silver Hittite
seal in the world is now in the Ashmolean
Museum.

The laugh, however, is often enough on
the other side. In my first *wanderjahr* I
was in camp with Mr. Ramsay in a wretched
Phrygian village far from the track of travellers. As we were striking the tents in the
morning a heavy-faced boy brought to my
companion a handful of bronze. He sorted
it rapidly on the palm of his hand, and
espied a single very rare coin of Hieropolis
among the Byzantine rubbish. Putting all in
the boy's outstretched hand again, he offered
half a dollar for the lot. Without hesitation
the boy accepted, gave back the handful,
took the ten piastres, and departed, while
my companion chuckled and went off among
the horses. Ten minutes later the boy re-
appeared, and, coming straight this time to
me, held out another handful of bronze, in
which I was astounded to see a second

example of the rare Hieropolitan type. Keeping the coins in my hand I offered another half-dollar : the boy refused, but eventually accepted a dollar. Hailing my companion, I informed him that he was now not the only man possessing a coin of Hieropolis, and showed him my purchase. "Let us compare," said he, emptying the pocket in which his bronze was jingling. He sorted the whole lot, felt in every pocket, but no coin of Hieropolis was there ; and for the rest of that day we had certain insoluble questions to debate,—who taught that heavy-faced Phrygian that one coin was rare and gave value to the whole lump? and to which buyer, now that the transaction was finished, did the coin belong?

CHAPTER II.

TRIALS OF A SCHOLAR.

Afium Karahissar—Sickness in a *khan*—Escape from the *khan*—Dogs and archæology—Fever and delay—Drought and famine — Water at last — Ilghin (Tyriæum)—The oriental mind—The ride abandoned —Konia (Iconium)—On the plains—Karaman—By waggon across Taurus — Thalassa! Thalassa!—Trials ended—A Levantine tramp.

I HAVE heard it hinted often that a Wandering Scholar's life is a disguised holiday. For all reply let me submit some notes of a ride from the Rock Monument region of Phrygia to the Cilician coast at Selefke. It was in 1887, and my first essay in Anatolia unaided by the great experience of Mr. W. M. Ramsay. My companion, H. A. Brown, had had a previous year's experience: he was no archæologist, and accompanied me in quest of adventure simply—a quest which had taken him alone into the wildest part of Albania, and led him at last to such a death as he used to covet most, with Major Wilson's little force in Matabeleland.

July 1st.—We said good-bye to Ramsay this morning at Beykoï, not without misgiving, for there is said to be famine this summer in the south country, and we are desperately ill-prepared for a scarcity. Our plan is to make our way to the southern sea at the least possible cost and with no incumbrances, by a route lying mostly off the main line of travel. Therefore we have no baggage-horse, and have left behind us tents, beds, most of our cooking utensils, and all our tinned stores, except a few sardines. We shall carry a little rice, sugar and tea, a change of raiment, surveying instruments and note-books in our saddle-bags, and in those of the servant whom we are to hire here at Afium Karahissar. One of R.'s men has come with us thus far for the look of the thing and to help us find another servant. We have had five hours' very hot ride over treeless plains and the rough causeways that are built

through the marsh outside this town, and
a halt of a few minutes only at one of those
little bath-houses so frequently seen in
Anatolia, built over a natural warm or
mineral spring. Several peasants were
paddling in opaque grey water covered
with a floating scum, and scooping now
and then a draught from the common bath!
We rode into Karahissar after midday, I
feeling feverish and limp and mighty indifferent to the jeers and occasional insults
with which all Christian strangers in this
fanatical town are greeted. The *khan* was
filled with the noisome stench of its cesspool,
and the best room we could procure is lined
with matting absolutely alive with bugs.

The first necessity was to procure money;
and after food and rest we set out for the
house of an Armenian who acts as agent
for the Ottoman Bank. I was provided
with a letter of advice and a cheque on the
Bank itself, and the Agent could not wriggle
out of cashing it, though he searched his
heart by the space of an hour. But B.'s
London cheque he rejected firmly, press-

ing us, however, the while to accept his
guidance round the town and dine at his
house. As we shall need his services to-
morrow in our search for a man and horse
we could hardly decline, and were led
rather a weary tramp round the outskirts
and up to the wonderful citadel, once
known as Acroenos, and a great Byzantine
stronghold. It stands on a pillar of basalt,
which springs up eight hundred feet sheer
from the plain, and can be reached only by
a stair cut in the rock. There are ruined
gates and bastions of small mortared
masonry, huge cisterns in the rock, a little
broken mosque (once a chapel), and some
rusty, dismantled guns. Dinner awaited
our return, a meal offered in all kindness,
but not tempting to a jaded appetite—
course after course of watery vegetables
smothered in sour cream, rice under the
same cream, stringy lamb's flesh garnished
with the same, and sad, sickly pastry. We
picked at them with our fingers, and the
kind host loaded our plates with tit-bits
selected by himself, rallying us that we ate

so little! Fleas swarmed, and the only
beverage on a thirsty night was a slightly
odorous and faint-tasting water. I crawled
back to the *khan*, and passed an evil night
of pain and fitful dozing among the insects
and heavy-hanging stenches.

July 2nd.—An interminable day. I was
too ill to dress till the morning was far
gone, and lay afterwards in the intervals
of the malady on the frowzy cushions,
faintly watching faces peering through the
bars of our window and a pushing crowd
offering antiques to Brown. The latter
bought a horse, saddle and all, in the
bazar for seven and a half pounds Turkish,
and engaged an old soldier, one Halil
Ibrahim, at three and a half dollars a
week to ride it behind us. Late in the
afternoon, feeling a little less ill, I accompanied B. through a jeering mob to the
Government house. We were received
with a mixture of suspicion and respect,
which became intelligible as soon as we
perceived, sitting abjectly at the lower end

of the daïs, Sultan Bey and his Circassian henchmen who entertained us last week while we were mapping and digging about the Tomb of Midas. They had been charged in fact with complicity in our reported search for gold ; and the governor, divided between greed and fear, had resolved, it seems, to let the Englishmen alone, but to make the poor Circassians disgorge. So our account of mere surveying and clearing earth from fallen sculptures was received with polite disdain, and we departed without coffee but with our papers ; but at what price the Bey may have purchased eventually his *congé* I know not. I fainted more than once in the evening and passed a half-delirious night.

July 3rd. Sunday.—When morning came I was very weak and low at the thought of another day of heat and stench and noise. Would it be impossible to go very gently about an hour's journey on our road to some quiet village with purer air ? The fancy began to possess me that I should

INTERIOR OF A *KHAN* AT AMASIA.

[To face p. 32.

never escape from this pestiferous *khan*
if not now ; and in any case we could but
try. The horses were brought out, the
saddle-bags packed, and, after much opium
and scalding milk, I was lifted into the
saddle, with a rug and an overcoat rolled
before and behind for support. At first
we proceeded but uncertainly, but, as the
town was left behind, something in the
pure morning air, something in the sense
of motion and escape put heart into
me again, and I kept on. The farther
we went, the better I became ; and
indeed I suppose my malady must have
been largely nervous, for in the end,
with the exception of a short halt at
a bridge, into whose balustrade a Roman
milestone and a Greek inscription were
built, I sat in the saddle for five hours,
and at midday reached Felleli, a large
half-deserted Turk village of the plain.
I could eat nothing, but I slept, and
so pulled myself round sufficiently to
copy in the afternoon the few inscribed
stones reported by the villagers. One

D

chanced to be in the courtyard of a house
whose owners were all out with the flocks
on the hills ; but two men offered to take
me in, if the dogs should prove to be not
about. Armed with sickles, we went to
the courtyard, and, finding it empty, sat
down before a small altar-stone built into
the house-front. The inscription was
upside down, and couched in that un-
familiar Phrygian language which was
used still in sepulchral imprecations as
late as the third century A.D.—the " speech
of Lycaonia," in which Paul spoke to the
men of Lystra ; and so I was long about
my task, and a house-dog, that had been
scavenging elsewhere, had time to return.
He made straight for us open-mouthed,
and, roused by his furious protest, three
of his fellows returned hotfoot. I finished
my copy in indecent haste, and, forming
square, we began a crab-like retreat
towards the gate, swinging sickles and
hurling stones at the maddened dogs,
who rushed and leapt from all sides at
once. There were about fifty yards to cover,

and I never had a livelier five minutes.
For all their swinging of sickles and hurling of stones both my native guards were
bitten about the legs and their clothing
was torn to ribbons, but they stuck to
me loyally, and succeeded in keeping the
shaggy brutes just at bay until we reached
the gate.   Beyond that point none of the
dogs pursued an inch. In the late afternoon
we took the road again, our path lightened
by a huge forest fire on the sides of Sultan
Dagh, and so came much exhausted to
a *khan* at Buluwadun sometime after
nightfall.

July 4th.—We are at the head of the
valley of the Phrygian Lakes, down which
Cyrus marched with his ten thousand
Greeks on the way to Cunaxa. Here lies
the site of Ipsus, and the great battle of
301 B.C., in which the greatest of the
Successors, Seleucus, won Alexander's
heritage from old Antigonus, was fought
probably on the grassy plain over which
we rode to-day: two mounds near Chai

perhaps conceal the slain. I recovered enough strength to-day to begin a rough route-map with prismatic compass and dead reckoning of pace. Such surveying is an irritating occupation at the best of times. If the compass reading is to approach accuracy, it cannot be taken from the saddle. You must dismount twenty times in a morning. If a horse be left loose he will sidle off the track to browse and get bogged ; if you slip your arm through his bridle, he jerks it up just as the needle was about to come to rest. He declines to stand to be remounted ; the ill-girthed saddle slips round unless you throw your heel over like lightning, and agility is not one's strongest point when weak and stiff from a malady hardly cured. So we crossed but slowly to Chai, and turned down beside, rather than on, the high road to Konia ; everyone seems to go beside and not on this road, which is grassgrown, its bridges rotten and often disconnected from the embankments. A little village came in sight on the flank of the mountain, and we turned up to examine it in hope of finding relics of Ipsus ; but no sooner had we arrived there than B. was seized with violent shivering fits, and it became patent that we must stay where we were for the night. We repaired to the village guest-house, and a weary afternoon ensued for me, who became the centre of a crowd of gaping rustics, B. lying torpid the while, and a wearier evening, for no food appeared until nigh ten o'clock, the headman's wife having long protested that she would not cook for *giaurs.*

5*th.*—Things have gone better to-day after a night rendered odorous at first by the proximity of a herd of buffaloes, goats, and sheep, penned in the courtyard of our house : we were disturbed also long ere light by the uneasy lowing of the kine and their futile but persistent efforts to get out to the pastures. A string of villages lay on our road, all bowered in fruit gardens, and we were received

courteously everywhere.   B. seems better,
having had a long mid-day rest at Sakli,
while I hunted up inscriptions of the old
bishopric of Julia in the blistering heat.
Finally we came at nightfall to a pretty
village, Deretchin, near the spot where
Xenophon saw the Fount of Midas.   A
cool stream rushes down before the guest-
house, and the peasants bring us apricots
and pears.   But our serious evening meal
once more has been long delayed, and
having tasted nothing all day except a
little unleavened bread and milk at sunrise
and some dry bread and rice at noon, we
feel unkindly towards Halil, who dodders
about and sits eternally like a true Turk,
and will bustle nobody.   B. overheard him
say at Sakli, "These are poor men ; the
one who was rich stayed behind" (*i.e.*,
Ramsay) ; and I fancy Halil chafes at long
rides and poor fare in such a service.

6*th.*—Overnight a man assured me
that there was a "stone lion" in the village,
but in the morning neither he nor his lion

were to be found. Then appeared others,
saying that a certain village, Uchkuyu, at
the head of the Aksheher Lake, was full of
" written stones." It happens to lie more
or less on the route I had intended to take,
so we started for it about 6.30, after the
usual breakfast of dry unleavened bread,
unrelieved this morning even by milk.
Our way lay over the marshy grass between the Lakes of Eber and Aksheher ;
much of the plain is cultivated and dotted
with summer camps of nomads, and two
sheets of water lay right and left, sparkling
under the low morning sun. There was
never a " written stone " to redeem the
arid nakedness of Uchkuyu, and after a
meal, hardly obtained, of barley meal
cooked in rancid butter, we came down
again to the reedy margin of the lake, and
rode all the afternoon along its north-
eastern bank, seeing no life but its
water-fowl, and hearing only the plash
of ripples, driven up by a westerly breeze.
The Turkman village we were seeking
receded always round successive corners

of the bluffs, and the sun had set a good
half hour ere we rode lamely into a small
settlement of Yuruk nomads.   There were
no men to be seen ; half the hovels were
tenantless, and women's heads peered fur-
tively a moment round doors and were
withdrawn hastily to an accompaniment of
the putting up of bars and shooting of
bolts.   In vain we knocked and asked for
water and a little bread ; the wolfdogs
answered, and forced us to retreat to the
outskirts of the village and tie up our
horses in a ruined byre, full of dung and
fleas.   The poor beasts found no provender
and no water, for the Lake was far away
in the dark, and there was no fountain to
be seen ; and we for our part shared a
single box of sardines with Halil.   Then
we lay down and waited for morning, B.
writhing in paroxysms of ague-pain shooting through back and loins.

7th.—The first dawn was hardly in the
sky when we were on the road again,
following a broad track in hope of a

kindlier village. Nor were we disappointed,
for after a few miles we sighted Korashli,
and an hour later were devouring a rancid
pilau. But water failed still ; the muddy
trickle of the village fountain just slaked
our own thirst, but was denied by the Turkmans to our horses. So we were forced
to press on without delay over the arid,
famine-stricken hills, B. complaining much
of his back the while, and the horses beginning to fail so much that we dismounted
and led them. We had tramped for a
little more than three hours when suddenly
the horses threw up their noses, and one,
jerking himself loose, broke into a hand
gallop and disappeared ahead. From the
next rise showed the village of Kumbulu,
and there the stampeded horse was found
at the fountain, painfully sucking up water
past his cruel spoon-bit. There was drink
in plenty and good hospitality withal, but
alas ! the *ayan*, who takes charge of
strangers, being a veteran of the Crimea,
declares that *he* knows Englishmen and
their tastes. They like roast fowl—no

rice, nor barley-meal, nor eggs for them!
We must wait an hour and a real English
meal should be put before us. We waited
an hour, and two, and three, and at last
a poor blackened thing appeared, which
we assaulted first with knives and then
tried to tear asunder, each holding to a
drumstick, and finally absorbed as best
we might in alternate sucks, each taking
a side!

8th.—A short day's ride by the reedy
Chaousji Lakes, haunt of flies innumerable,
and of many buffaloes, wallowing in black
slime; and we halted at Ilghin, the site of
Tyriaeum, where Cyrus reviewed his troops
in presence of the Cilician Queen, and the
Greeks scared the barbarians so sorely in
the sham fight. There were inscriptions
everywhere, in the mosque, in the fountains, and in the graveyards, and when B.
declared that he was too ill to go further,
and rain came on, I spent a happy enough
afternoon following an Armenian guide
into courtyards and among the tombs.

The Governor of Aksheher called upon us this evening in the *khan*—usually a haughty official, but for the nonce our very humble servant : for he arrested, it seems, a fortnight ago a Levantine Englishman, our Vice-Consul at Angora, for cruising in search of water-birds' eggs around the Lake of the Forty Martyrs, and is now on his way to Konia to answer the peremptory summons of his superior, Said Pasha, " Ingeliz Said," the most notorious Anglophile in Turkey. The poor man talked with nervous affability about antiquities, and Europe, and other things, which he neither cared for nor knew, and ended by soliciting our very gracious intercession, so soon as we should come to Konia.

9th.—B. gets no better ; dysenteric symptoms are supervening on his fever, and it is evident we must get to the sea as best we can, turning neither to the right nor the left. The heavy rain last night had made the morning air very chill,

and the plain a holding quagmire, through
which we floundered, huddled in our over-
coats.   At the foot of the hills B. collapsed
and we had to halt awhile.   Then we
pushed on for two hours more up earthy
paths which were still, or had hardly ceased
to be, watercourses, having on our right
flank the end of Sultan Dagh, shrouded in
black, low-hanging cloud.   There are more
Circassians about than is comfortable for
owners of horses.   At one o'clock we
reached Osmanjik, and I left B. in the
guest-house while I copied some late
Byzantine epitaphs.   On returning I found
him no better but very anxious to push
on ; so we started indeed, but after half
an hour his pain and state of collapse
left no alternative but to face about
and take up quarters at Osmanjik for
the night.   As a result I bagged one
more epitaph, and had one of those
weary, abortive rides which madden the
Western traveller.   A Turk presented
himself, offering to guide me to a hill
two hours away, where were " stones

covered with writing and with faces of
men and animals." *Bakshish* to depend
on results. As "Hittite" things are to
be looked for hereabouts, I mounted in
some hope, and followed for two good
hours through a couple of Circassian
villages up to the crown of a bare, cultivated hill. The Turk halted among loose
boulders : I looked about and demanded
where then were the stones with faces like
men ? He pointed to plough-marks on
one of the boulders, and I burst into oaths.
The man of the East only spread out his
hands in deprecation. Did I not want
written-stones ? There might have been
some here. God willed that there were
none. What was he to do ? I gulped
down my wrath and rode back sadder, but
a little wiser for another proof how incom-
prehensible is the East.

10*th, Sunday.*—Raining again and very
chill. B. seemed better for his rest, and
we pushed on past Kunderaz where were
many inscriptions, one in Phrygian, and

through dripping pine woods to the summit
of the pass.   The sky cleared and a gently
declining valley smiled before us, divided
by a bright, noisy stream.   Our mid-day
bread seemed sweeter than before, and a
nomad shepherd consented to call up his
nannies and sell us a pannikin of warm
milk.   As we near Konia there is more
life, and twice to-day we have had to draw
aside on the mountain paths to let long
strings of swaying, bearded camels jingle
past.   Strange how the horses hate these
familiar acquaintances !   A camel or a
wood waggon, deserted in the path, its
shafts in air, must be circumvented by
twenty yards at least.   We halted for
the night at Tatkoï and watched the
sun go down over the great earth-sea
of the Central Plains.   On the southern
horizon stood up, like blue islands, the
Kara Dagh and Hadji Baba Dagh, near
Karaman.   For the rest it was all one
misty level, save where far to the south-
east a line of points glittered on the chain
of Taurus.   Our meagre train and light

baggage placed us to-night under the unpleasant necessity of eating at the common
meal of the guest-house with three casual
wayfarers, God's creatures like ourselves,
and noways inclined to concede to the
owners of but three horses and a man the
privilege of privacy.

13*th*.—We have spent these three days
in Konia, which we reached in three hours
from Tatkoï. All thought of riding further
is at an end, for B. has become steadily
worse and cannot sit a horse. The only
resort is a native waggon, and I have
found a waggoner who will take us all to
Selefke, in five days, for fifteen dollars.
Heaven knows what the journey will be
like! for the waggon has no sort of springs,
and the road is said to be unmetalled.
We start to-morrow. Two of our horses
have been sold at ruinous loss owing partly
to the famine—they are said to be eating
rather than keeping horses in the villages
near—partly to a " ring " which took advantage of our necessities. The third

horse is still unsold and must trot behind
the waggon to Karaman. B. has been
very ill all the time, hardly able to last
through our interview with the Governor
on Tuesday, and generally lying somnolent
in the bug-ridden room of the *khan;* but
several people have been kind to us,
notably a Greek doctor, who would take
no fee, press it how we might, Mr. Keun,
representative of the Ottoman Bank, who
introduced us to Said Pasha, and M. Guise,
agent of a Smyrna mohair house. With
Said Pasha we had a long talk ; he is in
official exile for his English sympathies,
but they continue unabated. He was edu-
cated at Woolwich, speaks our language
admirably, and takes in, covertly through
the Bank agent, the weekly edition of the
Times. From his lips we learned our first
news of the Jubilee, and the progress of
Home Rule, of which, and of Mr. Gladstone,
he speaks much ill. He played great part in
the conclusion of the Cyprus Convention,
and since that event and our occupation
of Egypt, has been in disgrace, daily ex-

pecting a mandate to repair to Yemen, or, at best, Baghdad.

I have seen something of this old, old city, the first, according to one legend, to emerge after the Deluge. It saw Cyrus pass with his Greeks, and received St. Paul, and Frederick Barbarossa after his last great victory. Now it is dying, the half of it waste, and even the Seljuk walls, whose mud core, where the facing marbles have been stripped, displays the inverted impress of Greek and Latin inscriptions, are disappearing fast. There is very little left of Greek Iconium, except the Christian community at Sillé hard by, whose fore-fathers listened to St. Paul, and the Roman monolithic columns in the mosques ; but some Seljuk glories survive from the epoch when Konia was capital of the Empire of Roum. Most beautiful is the Mevlevi College with its tomb-mosque, where the Kilij Arslan's and Khaikhosru's are buried, each with his turban at his coffin head, beneath swinging silver lamps and tiles of priceless blue. One of its dervishes still girds the

E

Sultan with the sword of state on the occasion of his enthronement at Stambul. And in other mosques and among the ruins of the Palace are many white marble "stalactitic" canopies, characteristic of Moorish work also, and to be traced to a common source in Persia, although Moslems believe that they perpetuate the memory of an Arabian cavern where the Prophet hid himself in a time of trial. The town is said to be healthy, free from mosquitoes and fever, in spite of the marshy plain about it, and the refuse of three thousand years which leaks into its shallow wells. But trade does not come its way now, and the *bazars* are mean and half deserted, and a new block of Government offices stands up rather ostentatiously above the low mud roofs. The present Governor has done all in human power to better its state, and that of its province ; he has exacted honesty in tax gathering, assured public safety, reduced the undisciplined police to order, and begun a road to the sea. But he cannot remedy the Imperial arrange-

ment under which the Konia revenues are
charged with the Russian indemnity, nor
avert the consequences of official greed at
Stambul, thanks to which no reasonable
concession can be obtained for the exten-
sion of the Aidin railway to the Plains.

14*th.*—The waggon started early this
morning, and ran easily over the Plains ;
and B., lying full length on straw and
rugs, has passed the day better than any
for a fortnight past. There was nothing
to note on the great spotty level, except
shrivelled crops of barley, sad presage
of famine. Just at sunset we reached
Karkhan, our waggoner's native village,
where we have been treated as honoured
guests. *Pilau* mixed with dried grapes, a
roast lamb, and a curious thin paste, a
sort of damper, not unpalatable, were served
by our host and his sons. Rosewater to
wash hands and face before eating and
again after, and at the last admirable
coffee. Thus far all was silence and
dignity ; but no sooner were we seen to

be reclining comfortably, cigarette in hand, than all present fell on the remains of our meal at the lower end of the room like famished wolves ; and ere we had drawn three whiffs, they had cleared the tray, tipped a quart of water down their throats (the peasants drink like animals only after food), eructated an appreciative compliment to the bounteous provider of the feast, and begun to light up themselves !

15*th*.—On the Plains all day, but to-morrow we attack the Taurus. We have come to Karaman by way of the great mound of Gudelissin, which is probably the site of Derbe, but has now little enough to show that St. Paul saw, and by the dead town of Kassaba, with its mouldering Seljuk walls, and *khans*, and baths. Karaman is a pleasant little town of Turks, with a clear stream split into sparkling channels and conducted through many walled gardens. But its sun set at the Ottoman conquest, and only the shell of its Castle and the most exquisite stalactitic

portal of a divinity-school remind the
traveller that it was once the capital of the
Grand Karaman, who fills so large a place
in the story of the feudal kingdoms of
Cyprus and Armenia, and in the latest
glorious records of the Knights of Rhodes.
A little Armenian, superintendent of the
tobacco *régie*, has given us shelter and
food, but he means to cheat me of my
horse, and I can get no bid. We cannot
wait, nor can we well drag the beast over
Taurus, and I shall be forced to abandon
him after all. We hear that in this famine
year the district is full of broken men,
robbing and running contraband tobacco,
but we have too little to lose to be nervous. Indeed, shortness of cash has lost
me to-night a little clay tablet which may
be " Hittite"; and I have been able only
to take a wax impression.

16*th.*—We have climbed three thousand
feet, and the waggon is drawn aside for the
night by a little spring in a hidden hollow.
The spot is chosen to escape the stray

highwaymen who patrol the road. The day's journey has been rather weary. I for my part of course could walk up the long bare slopes, but B. had to lie still and be jolted over the boulders of the unfinished roadway. The scenery is all bald and grey, one dull slope of denuded crumbling rock, rolling up unbroken except by a chain of hillocks which range like huge *tumuli* on our left. No sign of human settlement, and hardly a trace of a human wanderer, and no water, except this trickling source, between a point two hours out of Karaman and Marah, which we are to reach to-morrow night. B. seems to have fallen into a state of utter collapse to-night, and to have lost heart, and I shall be more than thankful to see the sea.

17*th.*—At mid-day we reached the summit (6,100 feet), having traversed for ten miles a very desert of the damned, ridge upon ridge of rock, like the picked bones, of the earth. But once across the water-

shed we looked into a kinder world, and
long before reaching Marah were driving
under the pines. Unfortunately the descent is far worse for B.'s sore bones than
the ascent has been, standing to it indeed
as torture to acute discomfort. The waggon
takes flying leaps from boulder to boulder,
crashes across gullies, and rocks like a ship
at sea. Two dervishes in a second waggon
caught us up this morning, and at an awkward corner of the descent gave us a singular illustration of that Oriental immo-
bility, which we sometimes elevate into
stoicism, and sometimes, as fatalism, excuse.
A wheel went over the edge of the road
and their waggon was brought up short,
the horses plunging, and the edge of the
road beginning to break away. Below
was a sheer fall of some 200 feet. We
were a little way behind at the time, and
yelled to the dervishes to jump—but
neither they nor their waggoner stirred a
foot, and if we had not rushed up, and I
pulled the dervishes down by main force,
while our waggoner seized their horses'

heads, the three would have supped in Paradise!

Marah is nothing but a *khan*, half a dozen huts of nomadic shepherds, and some cabins for labourers employed on the road. The whilom overseer of these navvies has put himself and his hut at our disposal. He is a Greek of Greeks, clothed in assurance as in a garment, not clothed, indeed, in many other garments worth mentioning. He has a tattered Stràbo, I know not why or whence, and he has corrected me graciously on points of Cilician topography, imparting with easy confidence certain novel readings of his ancestral tongue. He bade us command him in everything, and call for whatever we might desire to eat or drink, for to ask in his house was to have! In the event he has eaten cheerfully a dinner procured and paid for at the *khan* by ourselves.

18*th.*—We left our host of last night, newly risen in the rags which serve him alike for night and day, and waving farewell

with a sort of bastard Parisian grace; and
the waggon went off leaping, pitching and
rocking out of one shadowy gorge into
another. The vegetation began to take a
sub-tropic character, arbutus, lentisk, and
oleander replacing the pine and the beech.
The cliffs on either hand reflect the heat
down on to the banks of verdure, and the
mists, rising nightly into the gorges from the
Cilician plain and the sea, feed their luxuri-
ance. But ever as we descended the heat
increased and the road gre worse. It was
just one o'clock when, as we emerged on to
an open shelf, a great shimmering expanse
opened below us, rising to a hazy horizon.
Thalassa! Thalassa! the sea at last! Even
the waggoner praised Allah it was the
sea, and was whipping round the curves
towards the brink of a great *cañon*, when a
sudden exclamation from me caused him to
check his horses. There had arisen above the
sky line the silhouette of a walled city, battle-
ments and towers outlined against the light;
and with a field-glass I could descry a gate
opening towards the opposite lip of the

gorge. What was it? No one had recorded a city hereabouts : was it Olba, so
often sought for ? I looked for a path
down the *cañon's* side, but there was none.
The waggon in any case could not cross
the gorge, and what could be done with
B. during the hours I must be away ? How
also were we to reach Selefke to-night, for
it was already late ? B. had but one idea
—the sea. What were ruins to a man with
ague in his bones and continual dysenteric
pain ? We debated long but found that
there was no alternative but to proceed,
and a turn of the road shut out this my first
fairy city, seen and lost like a castle in a
dream. During the last hour of the descent
we passed by a vast number of pillared
tombs choked with brushwood, the cemetery
of old Seleucia; and here and there, on commanding points, towers of a rude polygonal
masonry, which the pirates of the second
century B.C. built as refuges from the Roman
cruisers. On the right of our track reach
after reach of the Calycadnus shone far into
the folds of the hills. It was late in the after-

noon when the waggon, its wheels loosened
and its tilt in rags from frequent encounter
with overhanging boughs, rattled on to the
old peaked bridge below the castle of
Selefke, and an hour after dark ere we
heard the "longed-for plash of waves"
upon the beach of Aklimán.

And here ended our uncertainties,
and for B. the horrors of travel with
ague pains in his bones and dysentery
always threatening. We had, indeed, two
evil nights to pass in the squalid *scala*,
where the mosquitos rise in their millions
at sunset off the Calycadnus marsh, and
hot ripples lap on the shingle beneath a
heavy moon, like a sea in a disordered
dream. But the day between the nights
brought now no anxiety for a stage to be
travelled ere nightfall, but to B. rest on
our host's *divàn*, or better still the sea-
sand, which moulds itself to every curve
of a weary back. Early on the 20th a
steamer anchored in the bay, and, finding
that she was making the tour by Isken-

derun to Smyrna, we boarded her and obtained passage. The voyage lasted eight days, spent in running up to little ports like Castel Orýzo and Alaya and Adalia, names that one had known of old in romances of the Crusades. There we haggled for cargo with slimy native agents and took off cattle at nothing a head to chouse a rival Greek. A dirtier and more cockroach-infested craft I never sailed upon than that Levantine coaster, peace to her ribs! — they are whitening now on the Syrian coast, where she went quietly aground one calm night without loss to life and decently insured! The officers were Scotch and the crew Greek, and the latter understood the former according to the measure of vitriolic expletives. It might be said that the ship was worked wholly by profanity! The captain, meeting a friend at Iskenderun, looked on the Samian wine till he took a fever, and we did without him for the rest of the voyage; the cook, objecting to a Jew who was singing near his galley, sliced him from eye to

chin and had to be put in irons; and who
after that event cooked our greasy dinner I
never dared inquire.

Many are the ridiculous memories that
revive with the name of that disreput-
able tub that scavenged along the Levantine coasts, shipping contraband where
she could not get licensed cargo, and
defying pilots and the rules of ports; but
none funnier than of a certain squally night
on which we ran out of Iskenderun, the
whole sea red in the reflected light of a
forest fire. We were carrying on the
quarter deck a pasha's *harêm*, come from
the interior and probably new to the sea;
and as the ship pitched and rolled, and
wives and children and slaves fell very sick,
the oldest and stoutest duenna of them all,
starting up unveiled and half-clad, rushed to
the side and began to climb the rail, with the
evident purpose of leaping out of the
accursed ship somehow and some-whither.
But the old Scotch mate was too quick for
her: in an instant he had gripped her waist,
and for five minutes there was a Homeric

battle, he cursing gutturally as he held on like grim death, she hacking out behind, twining her disengaged hand in his hair, and defaming his maternal ancestors to the tenth generation.   The *harêm* shrieked at the awful spectacle of their comrade in the grasp of a man, but there was none to help, for the pasha was lying abject in his berth below, and we enjoyed the scene far too keenly to cut it short.   At the last she succumbed exhausted, and the old Scot bore her back like a sack to her bed.   At Adalia B. brewed himself a decoction of eucalyptus leaves, and whether because the nauseous draught had virtue, or because he believed that it had, he was recovering steadily when on July 28th our gallant craft dropped her anchor in Smyrna Bay.

CHAPTER III.

THE ANATOLIAN.

The Turk unspeakable—The Turk's womankind—The
peasant and the Padishah—Brigands and footpads—
Europeans and brigandage—The Smyrna *coup*—Islam
and the peasantry—The Yuruk—Nomadism—Survivors of Christianity—The Central Plains—A day on the
Plains—A garden of earth —Ottoman officialism—The
rule of the Aghas—Born bargainers—State of the peasantry—Peoples in youth and age—The Sick Man.

No more chastening instance than Anatolia could be desired by a moralist. The
Lamentation of Cicero over the desolate
cities of Hellas might be echoed now in Asia
Minor upon sites that were still great and
populous in his day; for its peoples
have shrunk within it like the lean and
slippered pantaloon. The walls of
Iconium enclose twice the space of Konia;
rare mud-hovels are scattered over the
Mound of holy Tyana; the squalor of
Kadin Khan has succeeded to Lystra, and

the filth of Armenian Pürk to Pompey's
Nicopolis. The list might be prolonged
at will : tombs of ignoble Moslem saints
attest some site of a Holy of Holies, and
periodic fairs alone bring back feeble life
to a market-place once crowded day by
day with the traders of half Asia. From
sea to sea vestiges of better days cover
the hillsides, tide-marks of the receding
levels of civilisation—strange hieroglyphs
and stranger sculptures of the early
pre-Aryan time ; stone lace-work on the
Phrygian tombs, simulating the carpet-veil
stretched before the other life ; Roman
aqueducts, theatres and roads, Byzantine
churches, and Armenian castles ; last of
all the Seljuk glories, the Mevlevi College
at Konia, with its delicate harmony of
marbles, its cool cloisters and fountains,
and the shade of its almond trees ; Sultan
Khan rotting alone in the Plains with a
portal fit for a palace, and the Divinity
Schools of Sivas and Karaman—these
reflect a sunset, since which there has been
no dawn.

And among all this slow death, the most

pathetic figure is the Anatolian "Turk" himself, "unspeakable" only in that he speaks so little. "Welcome, you have come!" "*Mahraba!*" he will say, and little else, unless in a garrulous mood he add, "Whence are you come?" Reply "From London," not necessarily because such is the case, but because he will know no other European town; say nothing of its five millions of inhabitants, for five thousand, or five hundred, or fifty would convey just as much or as little to his mind: far better to remark that in England eggs are sometimes two-pence each! "Dolt!" said a progressive *hoja* to a peasant who had asked me if London were indeed larger than his own tiny hamlet, "Who does not know that London is quite three times as big!"

This sort of "Turk unspeakable" is a slow-moving, slow-thinking rustic, who limits his speech to three tenses out of the sixty-four in his language, and his interests to the price of barley. Aliens, Greek, Armenian, Circassian, thrust him on one side and take his little parcel of land by

F

fraud or force—there is no real distinction in Anatolia. He appeals to no one, but dies by inches, begging at the door of the village mosque, until he may pass to that paradise of earthy joys which are to compensate so many earthly sorrows not foreseen by the Prophet. He is dignified in his slow way, strong and unclean as one of his own buffaloes, and clad in a shirt torn and blotched and tucked away into a leathern pouch-belt, from which he will disinter oddments of string and rags, flint and steel, and scraps of adamantine pemmican. Pendulous cotton breeches, patched and overpatched, are gathered clumsily above woollen cross garters that all Euphrates could not wash white, and with inherited knack he winds about his tasselless *tarbush* a blue rag or, if he be a *hoja*, a white, or haply a dubious green, should he claim to be one of the Prophet's myriad kin.

In energy and intelligence he takes rank a grade below his dog, who shares his profound and not altogether causeless suspicion of strangers, but attacks more

[*To face p.* 66.

PARTY IN THE TAURUS (BERÛT DAGH), JUNE, 1891

vivaciously and is reconciled more frankly.
Ask an Anatolian if any single thing, the
commonest in all the economy of nature,
is to be found in his village, and he will
say, "No"! before he has had time to
grasp your question. Describe a "written
stone": he has never seen one although
two Roman milestones may stand right
and left of his own hearthstone. None
the less he is a kindly creature enough,
but his wife ——! She clutches a coin and
spits at the giver: she denies you bread,
water, and shelter, offer what you will,
should the decision rest with her; no
suspicion of the virtues of Islam relieves
her fanaticism, and woe betide any traveller
who, riding tentless in summer, finds the
men gone to the hills, and their villages
left to the women!

Small blame after all to them if they are
ignorant shrews, seeing to what extent
they are treated as mere chattels of the
man, condemned to the hardest field work
and to walk while their lords ride. Even
Schopenhauer, who recommended "a little

ploughing" for the weaker sex, would have been staggered to see women carrying and laying the bricks of a rising house, watched by a ring of squatting men. I have seen a mother pass and repass a rapid rocky stream, carrying in succession a husband and two grown sons; and on the bare stones of Taurus all the women of a migrating horde trailing their bleeding feet after the camels, horses, and asses which bore their fathers, husbands, and brothers. God made woman out of man to be a helpmeet for him ; if the relation is ever inverted the man must be a slave, and for such in the eyes of Moslem peasants an English husband passes, who at a word from his wife rises and brings her a chair. Expostulate, and you will find the travelled Moslem turn upon you with a taunt against those who love and value their womenfolk so little that they put them within the reach of all other men. And, in truth, an Anatolian Turk never shows to better advantage than in some phases of family life, above all

with his children, those golden-haired
babies soon to be hardened by labour and
blunted by poverty, stagnating in the same
hovels that the fathers had inherited from
their fathers.

Travellers who assert that they "like
the Turk," mean such a "Turk" as this
Anatolian peasant. One is bound to like
him, if only for his courage and his sim-
plicity, and his blind fidelity and his loyalty.
Those villagers who fought so stubbornly
at Plevna and Shipka never received a
piastre, but, though they spit at the name
of Osman, who, say they, sat down in one
place that they might die, and invoke
Allah's curse on Suleiman, who sold them
in the Balkans, they say never a word
against the Padishah, whose conscription
is their chief woe, a woe from which the
much pitied Christian is free. When
British charity sends bread in British gun-
boats at a season of famine or earthquake,
the blessing of God is called not on our head,
but on the Padishah's. These 'Turks' are
honest, too, able, unlike the Arab, to with-

stand long temptation of gold, and gentlemen full of simple consideration for a traveller and just instinct of his needs. Alight at one of their guest-houses—in a Moslem village the house best built and furnished—and the elder commissioned by the community to attend on strangers busies himself at once to have the room swept, beds prepared, and due provision made for your horses. Presently arrive the notables, salaaming silently as they seat themselves round the walls, and again when settled. Coffee berries are produced, roasted in a wire basket, pounded, brought three times to the boil on the wood ashes, and served by a young man bowing hand on breast. The long silences are broken by a very few questions, until you show a sign, the slightest, of fatigue, when forthwith he of most dignity will rise, salaam once more, shuffle on his shoes below the *divan*, and without a word lead out the rest. Were they Christians you must have swept them out at midnight *vi et armis !*

The vices of the worst Moslem ruffian are

at least those of a conquering race; and, after all, ruffians are very rare among the peasantry of the central Plateau. In a lean year, when the leaves are on the trees and it is safe lying in the forests, villagers may take to the hills to avoid the tax-gatherers; but at the worst they will steal only cattle. Five such amateur horse-thieves hung about us once for some days in Cilicia, and might have given trouble had they not been forced by hunger to send two of their number into a Christian village for bread. The two were recognized, seized and marched away towards the nearest town; but they cut their bonds the first night with steel or silver, and vanished with the rest of the band. I have heard but of two regular outlaw chiefs in four years, of two men, that is to say, who kept the hills year by year; the one, Osman, ranged the province of Konia for some three summers with a dozen of his kidney, taking purses and lifting cattle; but he was of the romantic sort, delighting to rob

the Sultan's post or some sleek official, and
to give to the poor what he took from the
rich ; he would carry off maidens in order to
dower them, and dash on the best horse in
Anatolia through the midst of the troopers.
The other, an Armenian, was a ruffian
more truculent, who set the seal on his
fame by stopping a French vice-consul
near Aleppo and taking from him two
hundred pounds and all but the clothes
that decency requires.   There were strange
rumours abroad after the affair ; how the
consul's possessions were seen in official
houses at Aleppo, and of a pasha departing
suddenly for Yemen.   Certain it is the
brigand was not caught, for a little later he
was taking toll of all travellers on a road not
an hour's journey out of Kaisariyeh, and
he was still abroad in 1894 with a little
following of Circassians somewhere in
North Syria or Mesopotamia.

But such as Osman and the Armenian,
Chulu, do not hold captives to ransom ;
civilisation is not advanced enough in the interior, and brigandage, as the word is under-

stood usually, follows in the wake of loco-
motives and Greek newspapers. The robber
of the interior is a highwayman who will do
you no bodily hurt if you submit, and at
worst tie you to a tree to secure his own
escape. And even from the kidnappers of
the coast regions the European traveller
with no local connection has little to fear ;
for his movements are rapid and unknown, and he goes armed with weapons
for which the native entertains an inordi-
nate respect. His friends and relatives
are far away and his price is not certain,
and, most important of all, experience has
shown the brigand class that the capture
of a hundred native merchants, their children and their wives, will not cause one-
half the hue and cry that can be raised by
a consul with a gunboat at his back in the
bay. The wise brigand has no mind to be
besieged on a mountain side, where food is
scarce and water bad, for the sake of a
ransom he may never get, and, if got,
cannot enjoy. He learned the folly of
vaulting ambition in 1884, and the story,

well-remembered in all the region of
Smyrna, is worth telling again to illustrate
Ottoman methods and a type of brigandage
now hardly known. In that year two local
terrors, combining forces, conceived and
executed a mighty *coup.* Introducing
themselves by force and collusion into the
custom-house of a little *scala,* where a
coasting steamer was to touch at night-
time, they seized and gagged every one
who landed from her—man, woman, and
child—and carried them to the hills. But
the noise of the feat awoke the Ministry
of the Interior, and peremptory orders
came to Smyrna that no ransoms should
be paid, but the brigands' heads brought
in at any cost. The pursuit began hotly
enough, but Ottoman energy is seldom
equal to sustained effort, and as it cooled
the chiefs saw that there was room for hope.
They had still many of their prisoners,
and, working on the feelings of powerful
relatives in Smyrna, they concluded a
negotiation at last with the astounding
convention that, if they would give up

all their captives unransomed, they should themselves not only go scot free but be made policemen under their own leaders! So it was done; and these new guardians of the peace were sent inland.

For a while all went well; then rumours began to filter down to Smyrna of a reign of terror up the Mæander valley, of rapes and blackmailing and murders done in the name of the law; and ere long a second peremptory despatch from headquarters showed that the news had reached Stambul. What was to be done to capture these armed ruffians? A trap was laid, very obvious, but, it seems, sufficient. The new police were told that certain slanders had reached official ears in Smyrna, but the Vali was their firm friend. If they would disarm suspicion they must appear in Smyrna, and their appointments should be confirmed and their chiefs receive decorations. So they came down. Before entering the *serai* they stacked their rifles, and went up to the official presence with only pistols and sidearms. The Vali was cordial; decorations were promised and they turned to go, only to encounter a file of soldiers waiting in the corridor, and be bidden surrender! One chief and his followers threw up their hands, but the other, firing a pistol into the floor, sprang back and called on his men to stand by him. Stand by him they did with pistol and knife against rifle and bayonet until, his followers dead or bound and himself riddled with bullets, the chief ruffian reeled back to the Vali's room to avenge himself at least; but his Excellency had vanished by the window. Thus ended for a time the dare-devil type of Moslem brigand in the Smyrna province, and he has never revived as an organised terror.

Nevertheless, one must have a care; the armed shepherds near the coast are often potential robbers if they see the odds to be clearly in their favour. Near Smyrna in the autumn of 1887 mere amateurs, who expected no such prize, seized upon four members of a rich European family whom

Allah threw in their path. Similarly Mr. Macmillan was taken in the following year on the Mysian Olympus by shepherds, and killed, it seems, for what he had upon him, his amateur captors fearing to play for so high a stake as a ransom. There seems, however, to be but little general sympathy with the brigand, and an energetic governor, such as was Midhat at Smyrna, can make his province safe very quickly by timely severity. The most part of the peasantry are men of peace, needing no military force to coerce them, giving little occasion to the scanty police, and observing a *Pax Anatolica* for religion's sake. Their God is very real to these simple villagers, unspoiled by western freethought and not troubled with the subtleties of the Schools. Watch a group of them at prayer on the quarter-deck of a Levantine steamer; the European passengers stare and the sailors hustle past, but their attention is never distracted from the leader. With eyes downcast, with hands now raised to the ears now folded, erect, kneeling, bowing to the deck,

they intone the prayer, and rise dreamily
as men rise from a trance. Still more impressive is the united worship offered by a
line of wild men on a village green in
the moonlight. Whenever and wherever
they pray the peasants are with their God
as they know Him ; to them He is really
omnipresent and omnipotent, and for His
sake they practise, one and all, certain
simple virtues : age they reverence and
the chastity of women they respect ; they
abhor drunkenness, and through fourteen
torrid hours of a Ramazân day neither
eat, drink nor smoke, albeit at work in the
fields. The Prophet's injunction of hospitality even to the infidel successfully com-
bats fanaticism, and I have slept in a
mosque portico in Ramazân. Islam, by
the respect it secures to age, gives every
village the basis of communal government ;
and by the reverence that it prescribes for
the successor of God's Prophet it unites,
as no other force could unite, the heterogeneous elements that go to make up the
Ottoman Empire.

For even those elements that are
called by the common name of "Turk"
are themselves heterogeneous. Three
parts of the "Turks" of Anatolia never
came from Turkestan, but are children
of aborigines, Carians, Galatians, Phry-
gians, what you will, who accepted long
ago the militant gospel of monotheism.
Perhaps among descendants of old feudal
families or in ancient monastic cloisters
survive faint strains of the true Ottoman ;
but after so many centuries of intermarriage
with Caucasian and other alien races the
blood of that small military caste, which
came fittest out of the chaos of the fifteenth
century, must be mixed indeed. I take it
that, in many cases, the "Turk," most rightly
so called, is the despised *Yuruk*, the "wanderer," a name applied to the half-settled
population, roaming in summer among the
settled, but collected in the winter for the
most part into villages. They are not
gipsies, for those exist, distinct in type, in
many parts of the same land, and Yuruks do
not differ in anything but their name and

their unrest from many settled " Turks."
The truth seems to be that they are the
slowly-settling descendants of the pure
nomads who followed the Moslem conquerors at a distance ; they have various
pedigrees, many being true Turks, and
little by little, as they simmer down among
the long-settled aborigines, all will take the
name of honour, and in their turn despise
those who are still Yuruks. The process of
the change can be watched and is full of
interest; the scattered winter huts on the
hills gradually coalesce into a hill village ;
the summer wandering at large becomes a
definite migration to an invariable locality;
bit by bit even this outing becomes less
obligatory and less prolonged ; some
Yuruks never leave the village at all ;
others go and come, and the place of the
summer *yaila* is fixed hard by the village
itself. As they become rooted the nomads
part with their endogamous exclusiveness,
and those survivals of *Mutter-recht* and the
like which a wandering life renders necessary. The women lose their effrontery,

the men eliminate remnants of nature worship from their profession of Islam; they become agricultural as they cease to be pastoral, and insensibly they cross the divide and public parlance proclaims them no longer *Yuruk*.

But be it noted that nomadism dies very hard and long survives settlement. The practice of migrating to a *yaila* in summer is the most infallible sign that a village of " Turks " is not a village of converted aborigines; for *yailas* have practically no reason for existence on the high plateau where the nights are always cool— no reason sufficient, at least, to make a people, that has never been nomadic, take up its household gods. In the valley of the Saros, among the newly-settled Avshar tribes of Anti-Taurus, a village five thousand feet above sea level, surrounded by deep grass and abundant water, will be found abandoned in summer for a valley a few hundred feet higher with less pasturage and less water; and in 1890 we actually found the peasants of Saris camping out

G

in booths and tents not two hundred yards
from their village. They protested that
their house vermin drove them out; but
the houses could hardly have held creeping
things more innumerable than those summer tabernacles, and I make no doubt the
peasants' itch was of a more deep-seated
sort.

The Christians who survive on the
Western Plateau are dying too. Here is
no question of the Armenian, ineffaceable
as the Jew, for he is neither indigenous nor
numerous in the west; nor of the few
Greek traders who have pioneered a bastard civilisation from the coast; but of surviving communities of one blood, but not
one creed, with the aboriginal "Turks."
Why was the Koran not forced down the
throats of the Apollonian and Philomelian
Christians whose children keep the faith at
Olu Borlu and Permenda, near Aksheher?
How comes it that there is still a Greek
community at Sillé, an hour only from
Konia, once the capital of Roum, and that
the Turkish-speaking Christians of Cappa-

Photo by J. A. R. Munro.

[To face p. 83

THE BLUE COLLEGE (GYUK MEDRESSÉ) AT SIVAS.

dociaare lineal descendants of the flock of the Gregories and Basil ? The Seljuk Sultans were manifestly men of more liberal minds than the Emirs who succeeded them, or the fanatic tribe of Othman. In their eyes the Greek had his value ; the most beautiful of Seljuk gateways, that of the Blue School at Sivas, bears among its marble lacework and tiles, tinged by some lost art, an inscription recording that its architect was one Καλοιωάννης. A little community is living still on an island in the Lake of Egerdir, of which Byzantine chronicles record that it refused of its own motion in 1142 to receive the Christian hero, John Comnenus, finding the Sultan of Konia a better master. I paid a visit to it in 1890 with a companion, who is not more likely to forget than I the voyage in a rotten coracle, loaded till the gunwale had sunk an inch above water-level. A sea, which had come all the length of the great lake, was running abeam, and we set foot on the island with a profound thankfulness, overborne presently by the thought of return. A remnant of fifty Christian families huddles at one end of the island, where is a church served by two priests. No service is held except on the greatest festivals, and then in Turkish, for neither priest nor laity understand a word of Greek. The priests told us that the families became fewer every year; the fathers could teach their children nothing about their ancestral faith, for they knew nothing themselves; the Moslems were "eating them up." We had to force the church door, and brush dust and mould from a vellum service-book dated 1492. It was all like nothing so much as a visit to a deathbed.

And yet Nature is no niggard in Anatolia, but has granted early springs, brilliant summers, and sure rains—a climate like that of Central Europe. The western, northern, and southern hills still bear mighty forests, and their wealth of minerals has not been touched since Roman days. The Levant has no better harbours than the western bays of Ionia, and there is an easy road down the Mæander for the passage of the grain from that matchless corn-land, the Central Axylon Plain. Cartographers write this tract a Desert, and therefore that term must include an undulating treeless plain which sends up corn breast-high for the scratching of a Homeric plough. Fresh water is found everywhere at less than twenty feet, and deep grass grows in the marshy hollows through which streams creep to the central lake. When a land has not been called upon for centuries to produce, it is easy to rate its natural fertility too high, but, all allowance made, this Axylon with its warm days and fresh nights, its open, well-watered level and light soils, must be surely among the most desirable heritages of men.

I have seen many parts of it. Let me describe one August day on which we rode twelve hours, starting from Sultan Khan, the most gorgeous of the ruined Seljuk *caravanserais* on the road from Sivas to Konia. The morning had opened ill, for Circassian highwaymen, who had dogged us from Akserai, lifted our best horse out of a general stampede shortly before sunrise. We searched for hours among the *yailas* near, but, finding no trace, had to continue westwards in no contented mood. But ill-humour could not resist long the exhilarating influence of the salt breeze blown over the vast earth-sea which stretched a day's march behind us, and seemed limitless ahead. Eastwards the cone of an extinct volcano, Hassan Dagh, hung in mid-air like the last peak seen from ship-board, and our track could be descried for miles before us, dipping into the furrows and reappearing on the ridges, all clothed with a dusty scrub, under which showed sparse green leaves and grass. Presently we came on a deeper and wider hollow than ordinary, and climbed on to a Seljuk causeway laid over the marshy ground. A sun-lit mist on the plain ahead betrayed a village surrounded by threshing floors, and other clouds of golden chaff might be seen hanging here and there over isolated farms. Clear-skinned Turkmans, fan in hand, answered our queries, saying that they had come from winter-villages on the eastern hills, and that we should pass other *yailas* of their folk on our road ; and when we had satisfied their quick counter-questions, we rode on, meeting little variety. Now and again the track would dip down a low bluff and cross a marsh or slow stream crawling between soft banks, and then go up again on to the rolling waste, pock-marked with the burrows of innumerable prairie-dogs. A hare started from time to time, and red-legged partridges scuttled away beneath the scrub. As the sun passed to the south, the contracting horizon became vague and tremulous, and a far-seen mound rose up in air with a belt of atmosphere beneath. But for all that the heat did not oppress, and a salt breeze still blew southwards. We halted at a little village by the mound for the mid-day ; the breeze was dying now, and men and beasts huddled under any shade, the flocks head down, mere clusters of twitching backs. Two hours for repose, and then two hours more in the saddle, over a plain more lifeless than before, as far as a half-hidden village built among hummocky mounds which were strewn with old stones, here a cross, there an egg and tooth moulding, or the defaced medallion of a saint. Its name is Aghoren, "White Ruin," once Savatra, a city which coined its own money and must have equalled all the modern villages of the plain. We searched for inscriptions but in vain, and soon climbed again to the level, making for a line of low hillocks, marked chessboard wise with squares of cultivation. Two hours more and we were on their crest: ahead a dark patch showed in the eye of the low red sun. The plain began to take a purple hue and from piebald clusters, moving towards the gaunt swing-beams of a group of wells, came the tinkling of many bells. Tracks multiplied and ran into ours, and the broad road was penned pre-

sently between the earth fences of little
irrigated fields. We were nearing the
principal village of this part of the
plains, Suwarek, but the sun fell too
fast for us, and we had to ride down
its straggling streets in the pink dusk
of the afterglow.

Three to four days' journey from east
to west, eight to ten from south to north,
the great level stretches, but includes not
half the arable land of Anatolia. The
Cappadocian Plateau, rising to the east,
would bear as large a harvest a fortnight
later, besides grapes, and all kind of
fruit in its valleys. West lies an immense tract of hill and dale, larger again
than the Axylon, and its lower levels for
the most part are cleared and cultivated.
Verily Anatolia is one of the gardens of
the temperate earth, and perhaps some day
European colonists may return from the
lands of fever and fly, where their second
generation hardly holds its own and the
third fails, to take up this portion of their
more legitimate heritage.

Who else can arrest the Anatolian death ? Not the Ottoman rejuvenated by any political alchemy. His organs are wasted too far to be saved by any " reforms." Reforms ! How many have we pressed upon the Sick Man, and what is to show now ? What, indeed, could there be to show for the introduction of corporate responsibility where no western sense of individual responsibility exists ? The forms of a civilisation based on the equality of all men before the law have been imposed on men who, by religion and custom immemorial, respect persons. A system, pre-supposing development and progressive adaptation, is entrusted to a people who regard human initiative in change as an insult to the Creator. Centuries of slowly widened identification of the individual with the common claim of humanity lie behind the effective working of the European machine of government : in the Ottoman East the individual is considered alone ; there are no common claims of humanity.

Picture a mean, whitewashed barrack, with a long alignment of dingy panes, cracked and patched with paper. It is ten years old, but its unlevelled precinct remains a slough in winter, a dustpit in summer. The crazy doors open on a corridor, along whose walls runs an irregular dado of grease where frowsy heads have reposed, and the floor twinkles with fleas. Push aside the mat hanging before one of the little dens which open right and left, and look at the dozen men sitting on the cheap Manchester cottons of the *divan:* eleven have no business there, the twelfth, whose "office" this is, is doing no more than the eleven. An occasional coffee, a more frequent cigarette, the listless fingering of beads, make up the morning and the evening. It is the reduction to the absurdest of a western bureau, this parade of desks and ledgers and files. Coffee-cups and ash-trays monopolise the first ; and pages of the second are stopping the wind from a broken pane. A memorandum is penned slantwise on the folded knee and records are turned out on the floor from a wide-mouthed bag. In such dens as this all European travellers have had their weary experiences of Ottoman officialism, but they may reckon safely that for every hour and every piastre that they spend in getting merely a visa for a passport the poor native must spend days and pounds.

They are an evil unmixed, these semi-pauper officials, who all must live, and form a predatory class in direct contact with their prey, the peasantry. Things were better under the powerful Bureaucracy, which fell in the present reign ; then there was more local knowledge at headquarters and less harem intrigue ; a greater responsibility and a truer dignity in the official. Centralization is slow death in such an Empire as the Ottoman, whose nervous system of wires and roads is not half-developed, whose brain cannot adequately direct the members. In this heterogeneous loose-knit state such a feudal system as the rule of the *aghas* a century ago is perhaps best. The feudal lords at least were sensitive to the condition of the peasantry and were punished directly by their disorders. Justice at the city gate was done rudely, often venally, but at least done, and something was given back indirectly in the shape of alms and entertainment for what was taken. The great families, that could put a thousand horse in the field and sleep under their own roofs at every stage from Stambul to Baghdad, were doubtless too often brigands and foes to trade, but the Anatolian sighs now with the Old Pindari—

> I'd sooner be robbed by a tall man who showed me a yard of steel,
> Than be fleeced by a sneaking Baboo with a belted knave at his heel.

Now the descendants of the *aghas* who entertained Pococke, and Chandler, and Leake have perished utterly or lost their nobility and its obligations in official rank. Here and there an old man survives in ever increasing poverty, still eager to welcome the stranger, to offer all his

house, and serve him with his own hands;
but for the feudal chieftain, who will roast
whole sheep and bid godspeed with fifty
horsemen at his back, one must go to the
Kurds and Circassians.

The only form of government understood in the Ottoman East is immediate
personal government. The introduction of
an official system results merely in the mul-
tiplication of personal governors. Where
the governed supported one before, now
they support ten. They never complained
that they should have to support the
governor; they complain now that governors should be so many. What we of the
West term corruption and venality means
often not more to the East than a recognized system of *aliquid pro aliquo.* Fixed
stipends and centralized taxation are things
not less alien to Eastern tradition than the
equality of all men before Law that altereth
not. The peasant feels it no hardship to pay
directly for the services of the governor in
proportion to his own needs or the
governor's personal tariff; he likes to

have visible value for his money, one year
to pay nothing, the next to escape a visible
prison by paying treble, and he prefers,
on the whole, that his contributions should
vanish into visible pockets. The one
thing in the beginning of our administration of Cyprus disliked by the Cypriotes
more than the regularity of our taxation
was the incorruptibility of our local officials.
The Oriental is a born bargainer. Where
railways are new to him, as in Upper
Egypt, he will offer half as much for his
ticket as the booking-clerk demands, and
delay the train while he chaffers for ten
minutes at the window. Once I scornfully
asked a Greek trader, who had been haggling
over a certain bargain for a whole week and
gained thereby one piastre and a half on
the price first offered, at what he valued his
time? "My time!" he exclaimed, "what
else should I do with it?"

The Oriental, therefore, is probably happiest under a mildly "corrupt" and "oppres-
sive" Government. His indolence prefers
action that is inconstant; his gambling

instinct is gratified by inconsistency; and his fatalism secures him against any very acute mental misery. A piggish contentment with their lot has been remarked by all travellers as characterising the Anatolian peasantry, notwithstanding that there may be "corruption" abroad unbelievable except by a Russian. In 1891 at a certain centre of government I heard that the post of Provincial Receiver, tenable for two years only, at a stipend of 70 pounds Turkish, had been assigned lately to a candidate who offered 200 as entrance fee : the ex-Receiver was pressing a claim for a stray sum of 800 not yet paid over to him on an official bargain! It is commonly notorious that not one-third of the provincial credits for public works is spent on such works, and European would-be concessionaires of mining or railway undertakings make no secret of setting aside thousands out of subscribed capital for "commission" on the desired *firman.* There is withal "oppression" of the most arbitrary kind ; forced labour on

Government works with the accompaniment of the whip ; quartering of police at free rations on the poorest peasantry ; tax-gatherers seizing the plough-ox or the last sack of seed-corn ; sudden imprisonments and long detentions until money is paid, not for release, but for the preliminary privilege of trial.

But, all this notwithstanding, there is no misery apparent in most Anatolian villages. The peasant's standard of living is not high, his wants are few, and such as earth supplies to little labour. Ordinary taxation, which he hates, is very low ; extraordinary requisitions are not resented. Religion guarantees his exclusive possession of his women-folk, and a bare subsistence in any event. Not being highly developed, he does not feel acutely physical pain, but accepts a beating at the hands of a police trooper as a schoolboy takes a flogging. The gulf between prosperity and adversity is neither deep nor wide : the richest man of a village commonly lives in a similar house on like food and drink the same life

H

of manual labour as the poorest : a roof, four walls, bread, water and sexual joys are all that either craves. The luxuries of Anatolian life are its necessities, slightly more abundant.

These nations of the East are in their childhood, but it is their second childhood. They began to live before us, and in a climate where there is no strenuous battle to fight with Nature have developed racially, as they develop individually, more rapidly than we. The Egyptian was adult while we were in the Caves, and the Anatolian was living in great cities when we were setting up shapeless monoliths on Salisbury Plain. Now they are all very old and cannot put on again their youthful energy, or fall into the ways of a later generation. How seldom do we realise this truth in thought or speech! It is a commonplace to regard the Eastern nations as children, to whom we are schoolmasters. India is to be taught Western methods, Egypt set in the path of our own development, Turkey regenerated in our image. Vanity of all vanities! here is the sheerest alchemy! It is *we* that are the children of these fathers; we have learned of them, but we shall surpass and outlive them, and our development is not just what theirs has been, even as development of a second generation is never quite like that of the first. When we speak of educating India or Egypt we are the modern son who proposes to bring his father up to date. We are dominant in those lands for the sake not of their but our own development, and in order to use them as our own "stepping-stones to higher things." It is possibly not amiss for our own moral nature that we should hug an altruistic illusion at home, and we find little difficulty in doing so; but it is less easy abroad; no one who has been long in Egypt appears ever to talk about the "political education" of the Egyptians.

The Old Man in Anatolia neither craves nor can thrive on our strong meats. He has lost all keenness of desire, and is not equal to a new line of life. The young West takes him in hand, shakes him out of his lethargy, pushes him hither and thither, and makes fuller the evening of his life ; but likewise it makes it shorter. What more hopeful moral are we to draw from all the history of the concourse of civilised and uncivilised races ? The Turk, indeed, is a little less obviously effete than some other Orientals, because his upper class has been reinvigorated continually from younger stocks, the debt of the ruling families of Stambul to their Caucasian wives passing all estimation. But, none the less, those who knew the Turk before the War and know him now speak of manifest decline. He will never fight again as he fought then, for faith is weaker. His extremities no longer answer the call of the brain, Yemen in revolt, the Hejaz indifferent, Egypt separated, Kurdistan defiant, the Balkan provinces under a suzerainty not a sovereignty. And all these people—Arabs, Kurds, Bulgars—are "younger" than that aboriginal stock which formed the backbone of his armies twenty years ago. Most significant of all signs, he has lost heart himself. Already he foretells the stations in the retreat of the Crescent—Stambul to Brusa, Brusa to Aleppo, Aleppo to Baghdad ; and Moslem mothers tell their children that this or that will come to pass as surely as a cross will be seen again on Santa Sophía. And, be sure, the Turk will make no effort himself to arrest his own decay ; for as faith grows weaker, the original sin of fatalism waxes more strong—that fatalism which has been mistaken so often for a symptom of Islam, but preceded it and will survive.

CHAPTER IV.

THE GREAT RIVER EUPHRATES.

EVER since we had left Aintab the path had been falling insensibly towards a purple hollow, far seen in the east. Beyond interminable brown uplands rolled to the horizon, and all about stretched stony scrub, over which we rode hour after hour at that weary foot pace which travellers in such regions know only too well. Anxiously we looked for a glint of water to left or right or before, for between us and those brown slopes ran the fourth river of Para-

dise ; but up to midday and for two hours
after noon the arid monotony continued
unrelieved. The track seemed to have
ceased to fall and even to be taking an up-
ward cast again, when lo! the table-land
broke abrupt, as if cut with a giant's hatchet;
a sliding arc of brown water gleamed a
thousand feet below us—Euphrates at last!

As we scrambled down the cliff a mighty
roar rose up to meet us. The great river
was in spate, sweeping round a majestic
curve from the north and vanishing on a
contrary curve to the south, a fuller, broader
Rhine, rushing six miles an hour between
towering banks which had weathered to
fantastic pinnacles, and displaying a hundred metres' breadth of turbid flood, boiling in mid-stream over sunken rocks. It
is no child's play to cross it at any season,
and least of all when the snows are coming
down ; but cross we must if we were to go
north, for on the right bank we should encounter presently a great tributary, unford-
able, and without ferry or bridge.

A single boat of strange build was
moored to the bank opposite, beneath the

gardens of a little white town built terrace-
wise up the precipice. We holloaed lustily,
and leisurely one by one a crew mustered.
The boat was manned, shoved off, and
whirled away incontinently out of our sight
down the seething current. Evidently no
more would be seen of her for an hour or
more, and we lunched at leisure until a
knot of bare-legged Kurds hove in sight
labouring at a rope's end, and we were
bidden follow still half a mile up stream.
The boat was a primitive craft, nearly flat-
bottomed and very broad in the beam, her
planks nailed clinkerwise on a spare frame-
work, abhorrent of any symmetry of shape
or disposition. Square low bows admitted
of the embarkation of horses, and her stern
ended in a high poop and antediluvian
rudder, which projected far into the stream
its monstrous fishtail. No instruments of
propulsion were visible except two poles,
assuredly not for purposes of punting in so
deep a river. Our horses had never seen
a boat ; but being fortunately less imagin-
ative than the steeds of Europe, and
somewhat irresponsive to outward im

pressions after a fortnight on the hard
high road, came in over the bows
without much ado, and were penned up
head to tail with a stout bar behind. As
the tub took in her load she began to leak
ominously, but the crew made little of it,
plugged a seam here and there with the
end of a turban-cloth, and advised us to
stand as high as we could. Now we are
ready! Two men seize the poles and two
more the tiller, the shoreman pays out
the rope, everybody shouts, and away we
swing down stream, the leakage swishing
across and across the horses' hoofs. The
bowmen lug frantically at their blade-
less poles, using them as oars and obviously with effect; the men at the rudder
work its tail from side to side like a
stern-oar, yelling all the while above the
screams of the stallions. Round comes
the tiller! down duck our heads, or they
would be broken! we must hang on the
gunwale like bats, our toes drawn up
out of reach of the plunging hoofs. In
sober fact it was all perilous enough, for
many accidents have happened ere now

to these crazy craft; but before we had collected ourselves to think about danger we were spinning in a back eddy and brought up with a bump against the Mesopotamian shore.

We found ourselves landed among the gardens of a tiny white town, most of whose population came down presently to inspect us on the river bank. There was a new coffee-shop with a clean upper chamber in which we were lodged; a sleepy little *bazar* where edibles were kept from year to year until eaten; and a fat Governor, who received us on the roof of his house, sitting on a low wooden stool. He was a small man every way, but as overseer of roads or in some such capacity had been in most parts of Asiatic Turkey, and his exuberant goodwill was to be bought by anyone who would trot out his geographical knowledge before the gaping Kurds. The town is new: Khalfat used to be a little village under its own chieftain in the days when a Kurdish prince ruled his feudatories from the castle of Rum-Kalé, an hour distant up the stream. Above the Rhineland gorge of Khalfat lies a corner of Kurdistan ; village after village is held by the handsome brown-white men with narrow eyes and crisp hair curling over broad, low brows, who speak a tongue mocked by the Turks as a twittering of birds, but to our ears full of uncertain Aryan echoes. Their women crowd about the stranger unveiled, and laughing allow him to see their handsome faces and the strange devices tattooed on their forearms ; but he must confine himself to an interest coldly scientific, for the men are the most jealous of any in the East, and for that reason slow to welcome a guest. We always, however, made a point of disregarding their polite protestations of inability to entertain us fitly, and found them hospitable after all when assured of our good faith.

When Von Moltke was writing his famous letters from Malatia, the Sultan's writ did not run in all this region, and the hostility of the Kurdish Beys increased mightily the difficulties of Hafiz

Pasha in his vain effort to drive the army of Mehemet Ali out of Syria, and contributed to his crowning disaster at neighbouring Nisib. But since the Crimean War all has been changed; and the Turk's emphatic settlement of thus much of the Kurdish question in his own favour is a fact noteworthy and significant. These men about Khalfat are now no longer "fierce fighting Kurds." In facial type and speech they group with the northern tribes, but are become already true Moslems who do not sacrifice on stone altars nor set up a stone as an outward and visible sign between themselves and Mecca, as I have seen their folk do in the Taurus; and, shades of the princes of Rum-Kalé! these children of their feudatories are reputed the most easily squeezed of all taxpayers in Ottoman Asia! The plateau, on which they have been settled this century past, is very fat; agriculture tempted them in the day of their independence, until they came to have too much to lose, and, vigorously handled

these thirty years, their feudal chiefs have
resigned, bit by bit, all their administrative functions. I take it that in such
using of natural influences would lie also
the only solution of the northern Kurdish
question possible for the Turk. Whenever and wherever the Ottoman Government is strong enough, it must undertake
wholesale deportation of the Kurdish tribes
to the Plains, imitating the practice of the
old Persians, and lately of ourselves in
north-western Hindustan. The Turks
themselves have made, indeed, a success-
ful experiment of this high-handed sort in
the region of Amanus, and now there is no
Kurdish question there. A governor or
a marshal who will use vigorously the
Fourth Army Corps, ignoring the Armenians and the Russians for a season, might
put an end in a single strenuous campaign
to the Kurdish difficulty from Erzinjian
to Van. The whole history of the East
is one of the peaceful development—decline, if you will—of barbarian mountaineers
descended to the Plains : assist the process,

provide that the plain be out of sight of the mountain, and the most intractable brigands in less than a generation become the most tractable tillers of the soil.

By the fourth morning we had ridden across a corner of this Kurdish region and reached the river's bank again at the point where the great Eastern road in Strabo's time set out towards India. The treeless uplands had brought us only long blank days, with nothing to shoot and nothing to see, except here and there a brown reach of the river, flashing for a moment between low cliffs. Kurd village had succeeded to Kurd village, each with its little guard-house of the excise, standing up among squat hovels, half subterranean. The same black-haired, gaudily dressed women, the same naked urchins, the same deep cornlands in the valleys, and milky streams descending from scrub-clad hills, made up the picture always ; and, tired of such easy travel, we hailed the ferry of Samsat, hoping for fortune more various on the right bank. A boat even more infirm

THE EUPHRATES AT SAMSAT (SAMOSATA).

[*To face p.* 111.

and manned by a crew even less skilful
than at Khalfat put us all ashore on
the marshes below Samsat, thanking Pro-
vidence, and we found a welcome in the
house of Yusuf Agha, one of the very last
of the Kurdish Beys in this region.

Here was patriarchal feudalism as it used
to be ; we were received by an old man,
whose word is never questioned, and whose
entry brings every man to his feet. He
dispenses hospitality, morning and night,
to all comers ; no one in the little village
but tends his herds, ploughs his fields, and
dwells beneath his shadow ; and, with a
sweet dignity befitting his dying order, he
placed his house and all in it at our plea-
sure for two days and nights. Samosata,
the key of the principal crossing of
Euphrates, capital of Commagenian kings,
station of a Legion, birthplace of Lucian
and of Paul the heresiarch, has fallen very
low. Scarce a hundred huts huddle in
one corner of the old site, marked now by
the line of the Roman fosse, by a ruined
river wall and by gaunt fragments of

rubble. A black stone with "Hittite" inscription, defaced even more hopelessly than other monuments of its class, lies face downwards where the flocks are milked; two tiles of the "Steadfast Flavian Legion XVI." and a soldier's dedicatory altar were disinterred for us from heaps of kitchen refuse; there are some trivial Greek inscriptions in mud-walls and in the castle-ruins, — and that is all of Samosata.

But, pushing northwards up the river bank, we came on notable ruins of an aqueduct, straddling over the mouths of tributary gullies. Von Moltke had reported ancient works of defence, closing the lateral valleys on the right bank. This aqueduct was what he saw. Its arches have been half filled with coarse masonry by later hands, but the addition makes the aqueduct no more defensible than before (for it is commanded on all sides), and seems to have been intended only to strengthen the water-way. For nearly twenty miles the clearer stream of the tributary, which is now

called Kiakhta Chai, was conducted thus
to Samosata, though the sweet waters of
Euphrates ran by the very walls. What
the modern peasant is content to drink
was not good enough for the contempora-
ries of Lucian.

The Taurus, whose snowy summits had
been nearing us day by day, now began
to close in on the river. The stream,
no longer oozing among reedy islands,
as at Samsat, came foaming down rock-
ladders, beaten from side to side of its
channel by the jutting cliffs. The road
became a footpath, then a goat-track, and
at last broke off altogether on the
face of a precipice fifty feet above a
tormented eddy of the river. It was
an awkward moment : the horses had to
be turned in their own tracks, and nothing
but the stolid docility of the weary beasts
saved us from disaster. We made a *dé-
tour* through the hills and came down to
the river again, but it was idle to perse-
vere in face of the assurances of the
Kurds that not even a goat could go much

I

farther : and when we reached the Kiakhta Chai we had made up our minds to strike due north and rejoin the Great River above Malatia.

A reckless Kurd guided us across the mouth of the Kiakhta Chai late on a stormy afternoon. The melted snows of Taurus were coming down in wild yellow eddies, and the stream ran from bank to bank a quarter of a mile wide, with here and there a shoal, and everywhere a possibility of quicksand. We plunged from shallow to deep, following what seemed the wantonness of the guide, but really his cautious avoiding of treacherous bottom ; and, as we turned every now and again with the current running five miles an hour at our saddle-flaps, we seemed to be backing vainly against the flood, and lost all sense of independent motion or direction. It was a dizzy half-hour's experience, and horses and riders alike very thankfully struggled out at last on to a stationary world.

That night we lay at a Kurdish hamlet,

where even a glass bottle was passed from hand to hand in silent wonder, and rode all the next day over the rising foot-hills towards the base of the huge pyramid of Nimrud Dagh, whereon is the sepulchral tumulus of Antiochus I. of Samosata. He was a petty king, this Seleucid, who presumed to oppose for a moment the first Roman army that watered its horses in Euphrates; and in the event he had to submit swiftly and utterly, and end his days an obedient client of the great Republic, the shadow' of whose coming Empire was cast already far into Asia. But in his death he is exalted above all the Great Kings, lying there on the topmost peak of a mountain, surrounded by rude *colossi* of his divine ancestors, their feet in the snow and their faces looking out over Commagene and far across Euphrates to the Mesopotamian desert.*

* This extraordinary monument, surely the most grandly placed in the world, was discovered by Ch. Sester in 1881, and described admirably by Messrs. Humann and Puchstein in their *Reisen in Nordsyrien*, &c. It is strange that it has attracted so little general attention.

In the wild valley below is a monument of his conquerors, hardly less stupendous. The frontier road of the Empire had to be carried over a fork of the Kiakhta river perhaps, if this valley was traversed also by the royal road of the Persians (as is possible), and by the "common road of all who go up to the East," described by Strabo, there was a still earlier bridge; but in any case the Romans built it anew, and it stands still, with hardly a stone displaced. The single arch spans one hundred and twelve feet, and the keystone is fifty-six feet above mean water-level. Three columns are erect at the ends of the balustrade, graven with dedications by the four cities of Commagene to the Emperor Septimius Severus, his wife, and his son Caracalla: the fourth column, which bore Geta's name, was removed after his murder. Four tablets and four altars, built into the balustrade, record the Emperor's restoration—a restoration of such a sort that after seventeen hundred years there is hardly a crack or a hole. Nothing could

ROMAN BRIDGE NEAR KIAKHTA.

[To face p. 116.

demonstrate better how the long arm of
the Empire reached to its uttermost con-
fines, than this monument in a remote
Commagenian gorge ; and that fine comparison of the Roman Imperial system to one
of its own buildings, more costly and more
painful to destroy than to construct, has no
better illustration than the Kiakhta bridge.
Now the roadway serves for Kurdish
goats to trot from one pasturage to another.

We were come at last to the foot of the
Tauric wall : by which pass should we
cross ? I detected the fancied ruin of a highway going up from the bridge into the Taurus, and resolved to follow it. The Cilician
muleteers struck : they had come, they said,
far enough from their wives without going
where their beasts would perish among
the rocks, and themselves be killed by the
Kurds ! And did we not know that there
was a " road of peace " nearer the river ?
They called Heaven to witness they would
go by no other ! I swore they should go
my way or depart unpaid ; and there came

in an evil hour an Armenian, saying that my road was fair going. So we started. No difficulty on the first ridge, thickly set with green arbutus and lentisk shrubs, none for us horsemen among the pines on the second, although rocks jutted awkwardly and the path narrowed to no more than six inches. But it proved a different story for the baggage-mules, lagging far behind. One was forced over the edge and rolled to the stream below, but the loads broke his fall. Twice the packs had to be unloaded, ported round an awkward corner and reloaded; and all seven muleteers were weeping and cursing by turns when they struggled up at last, two hours in arrear. It seemed worse now to go back than forward, although our "ancient roadway" had vanished long ago, and so we pushed on, here bracing up a mule as he rounded a sharp corner, there disentangling another from the boughs of a pine. Presently the path dipped (for we were as yet on the spurs only) into a gorge a thousand feet deep, and the caravan,

having shuffled and slid somehow to the
bottom, came to a halt, that the loads of
the quivering beasts might be readjusted.
It was as lovely a scene at that point as
heart could desire; fold on fold of dark
pine forest, rolling up this side and that
of a mountain torrent to a huge peak,
glittering in the bluest of skies : but, paradise or no, we could not afford to linger,
and with infinite labour but no further
accident climbed out of the gorge again to a
camping-ground on a little patch of grass,
exposed among the lowest of the melting
snows. Things had not gone well, but
they might have been worse ; we had made
only five native hours in ten, and the night
came up cruelly cold on that knife-edge
five thousand feet high : but there were
pine logs in plenty to warm us, and Kurdish shepherds at hand to bring forage and
milk and eggs. In the mountains the
Kurdish tribes are less tame and less
orthodox than in the plains, clinging to stone
altars and strange crosses, and vicarious
witch-dolls set up over the graves of their

dead, and very wild eyes peer from under
their huge turbans built up of kerchiefs, as
many, it is said, as the wearer has years.
But, nevertheless, they are not really a
formidable folk, but just rude shepherds
and woodcutters, leading a half nomadic
life, and bartering in the *bazars* of Malatia
and Marash with the dwellers on the
plains.

The guides spoke of trouble to come, for
we were not yet at the summit, and there
was still much snow.   It was now late
spring, and snow in such a latitude at that
season must mean rotten bridges over
gullies, and soft deep holes and doubtful
fords.   So in fact the event was to prove.
Horse after horse on the second day broke
through the treacherous crust; girths
snapped, saddlebags scattered their precious contents, loads collapsed, and the
frightened animals kicked their way out of
one hole into another.   Bred in the plains,
they had probably never seen snow; and
presently had to be flogged on to the
smallest patch of it.   Poor beasts! they

will never have a worse three hours!
Now one glissaded down a snow-slope,
now another nearly drowned self and rider
in snow water; we seemed but to escape
from one evil into a worse, until the muleteers had exhausted their vocabulary of
execration and become reduced to one
monotonous plaint, "We are being taken
into Hell; but what can we do!" But
by better or worse paths, by this device
and by that, we got over the watershed by
noon, and struck at last a broader path
below the snow-line. The forests of
the southern slopes were succeeded by
bare grassy shelves, presaging that treeless desolation with which travellers in
central Anatolia are familiar. Not that
there was really desolation as yet; water
was abundant and the herbage deep
and lush, and the broader tracks, as well
as frequent villages, half seen in side
valleys, spoke to a population far more
numerous than on the savage Commagenian side. And if the open glades
through which we were riding were

monotonous enough, there were distant
prospects all around of a grander character; the huge snow-streaked spine of
the main chain rose still on our left hand;
a billowy sea of shaggy ridges fell away on
the right towards the cleft through which
Euphrates was rushing unseen, and, as we
emerged on to the open, a glittering saw
rose on the horizon before us. In ignorance of the bearings I thought it must be
Anti-Taurus, although it looked to be a
range more tremendous than I remembered
the Bimboa Dagh to have seemed three
years before; but in the event it proved to
be that famous Kurdish stronghold, the
Dersim Dagh, situated on the farther
bank of Euphrates, over a hundred miles
from the pass in which we were. That
night we reached late and slept at a
Kurdish farm within sight of the Great
River again, and came in peace to Malatia
on the third day.

Malatia is the half-way house from
Stambul to Baghdad, but it seemed
ominously still—no camel trains jangled

through the streets, no wagon-tilts blocked
the great courtyard of the *khan*, no
colluvies gentium was crowding its *bazars*.
The truth was soon learned—the great
post-road from Stambul was closed a few
hours to the north by a quarantine *cordon*.
We had heard rumours already that cholera
was in Sivas, but had not believed them, for
the plague had been unknown before on the
plateau of Asia Minor. And worse news
was to come; a Kurdish village two hours
distant from us was suspect likewise, and
Malatia itself had been declared infected
for ten days. None of us had a mind for
quarantine, I least of all, who had experienced five days' detention three years
before. At that time cholera was in
Aleppo, and my party was caught on the
frontier of the province trying to go north.
The soldiers forced us to camp beneath an
August sun at midday on a bare hill-side
without a green thing in our sight; no
fresh food could be procured for twenty-
four hours, and no water better than that
of a stagnant pool, in which Kurdish goats

drank and buffaloes wallowed at evening and noon.   A motley crowd of miserable suspects were stewing in two black tents hard by, some suffering from a colourable imitation of cholera, due to the foul water, and many long overdue to depart.   Ten days was the legal term, but in the absence of any doctor who might sign clean bills of health some poor wretches had waited already for fifteen days.   During the first afternoon and night we were guarded in the most approved manner, Martini to right and Martini to left; all money was passed through vinegar, and a letter to the local Governor fumigated so thoroughly that on its receipt the official gorge must have risen.   Our tobacco, however, was reported somewhat superior to the local supply, and next morning the guards foraged for us and forgot to sulphurate their own *bakshish*.   On the third day we began to trade directly with the Kurds, while the *cordon* looked away.   The fourth sunrise brought out a fat Armenian doctor ; fleas and ticks in the guard-tent gave him riotous welcome, and the soldiers made a point of proffering the foulest water of the pool after his long ride. He spat hastily and preferred thirst. The afternoon was passed in argument; on the morrow camp was moved to better water, and by midday, the thermometer in our tent registering 110° Fahr., the good doctor's mind became amenable to reason. As a result of various forms of reasoning we were shut on the sixth morning ten at a time into a bell-tent: through the only air-hole a pan of burning sulphur was introduced, whereupon we burst out incontinently among uprooted pegs and broken guide-ropes! the doctor signed certificates that we had kept ten days quarantine and been disinfected thoroughly, and, that done, accompanied by a motley crowd, drawn from half the races of Western Asia and astride on all manner of beasts, we resumed our way to the north. These quarantine *cordons* have become an unmitigated, because ever-recurring, curse. The trade of the Syrian cities has never recovered from the re-

strictions of 1890 and 1891, and the Black
Sea ports will not revive for ten years
after 1894. While the small fish are
netted the big are often allowed to pass ;
and infection meets with little or no im-
pediment where commerce is throttled.

On the present occasion, however, we
had neither to bribe nor to bluster, for,
after three days spent in the garden-town,
where the Malatiotes congregate now, and
two in the ruined city which they abandoned in 1838 to Hafiz Pasha's army, we
learned certain tidings that there was no
cordon established yet on the Arabkir road.
Folding our tents swiftly and silently, we
rode through the gap, and doubled warily
to the bank of the river north of the fords
of the Kuruchai. It was a lucky escape,
for already we were tired of Malatia, of
watching Armenians sell and Kurds buy
in its squalid *bazars*, and receiving all conditions of men in an upper chamber of the
khan. One visitor, indeed, had been out
of the common run, an Epirote Turk, once
a petty police officer of Gordon's at Khar-

tum, and captured there by the Mahdi. He had not witnessed his master's murder, being already in bonds, which he bore for three years until, being sent up into Darfur, he made his escape on foot to Zanzibar, and came by way of Bombay and Baghdad to Malatia. We found it difficult to extract from his slow intelligence anything beyond general descriptions of the sorry state and destruction of the captured Khartum and of his own sufferings as a slave at Omdurman. He thought little of the Mahdi himself, whom he had arrested as a youth for the theft of a boat—he was " a nothing," "*a two-para man.*"

When we reached the Great River again it was swinging round an elbow a few miles below Chermuk, not now a ladder of tumultuous rapids, but a full even flood, half a mile from bank to bank. A few shaggy islands broke the stream, and from one to another a naked Kurd was navigating on a distended goat-hide. He halted to readjust his float on the shingly beach of an islet, tied up the leg-holes more tightly, and then, slipping a loop of hide over his head, waded staggering into the strong current. As the water came above his knees he sprawled forwards on the belly of the float, and pushing off with his feet was soon no more than a black speck on the yellow sea. The Kurds carry their grain in this fashion to down-river markets, drifting breast high in the flood by day and at night sleeping on a shelving beach.

Above Chermuk the scene becomes mountainous again, and the river curves in craggy meanders. Halting at a dizzy height above it, we saw again to the north that white saw which we had spied from the Taurus. The famous or infamous Dersim is the huge *massif* which divides the fork of Euphrates and harbours the most defiant rebels in Turkey,—the true Carduchi of Xenophon, an old race, which obeys none but its own tribal chiefs and worships still an unknown God, who is not the God of Islam. The Turks have surrounded them with a ring of forts from Kharput to Erzinjian, but have not succeeded in breaking

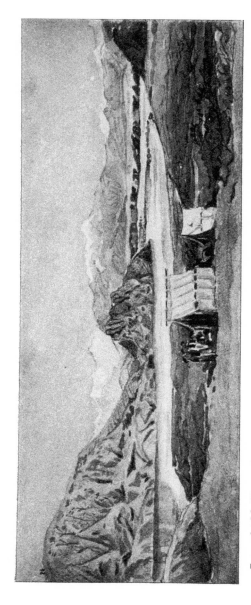

From a sketch by *Viscount Encombe*.

VIEW OF THE EUPHRATES LOOKING SOUTH TOWARDS TAURUS FROM KILISIK.

their stubborn backs. Their tremendous stronghold is entered from the north by defiles more than nine thousand feet above sea level, and the Kurds reck little of the Fourth Army Corps, whose bugles they can hear across the plain of Erzinjian. In the autumn of 1893 an attempt was made by a colonel with three officers and two hundred rank and file to collect arrears of dues from the outskirts of the Dersim ; the wretched soldiers, with no efficient commissariat and clad for the plains, were guided from pass to pass, broken with hunger and cold. At the last the Kurds gathered on the cliffs of a narrow gorge with their long rifles and with poised rocks and began the work of death, and no man of the detachment, officer or private, ever returned to Erzinjian.

Our road was not to lie among these mountains, but on the bank opposite to that to which their foothills fall, through villages of Armenians and " Turks," the latter long settled, peaceable and prosperous. There is not a trace of nomadism in all this region ;

K

the "Turks" are settled agriculturists, who do not flit in summer to a *yaila*, and their facial type is indistinguishable from the Armenian. Indeed, they are doubtless originally of the same blood—a converted population remaining throughout Armenia among those that have kept the faith. Such "Turks" are found all round the elbow of the Eastern Euphrates; about Divrik their villages alternate with Christian, but above Pingan on the right bank they cluster more thickly together. "Turks" form almost the whole population of Kemakh and a moiety of that of Erzinjian; and the same thin-featured, white-skinned type is found everywhere northwards until merged in the Georgian physiognomy of the Lazis. I cannot speak for Eastern Turkish Armenia, the region of Van, Bitlis, Mazgird, and Erzerum, but would dare wager that there too, wherever a rooted Moslem population, calling itself "Turk," exists among the Christians and the various tribes of Kurds, it is mainly of Armenian stock.

An hour above the strait of Keban Maden, where the stream is pent between cliffs not two hundred yards asunder, the two main waters which make the Great River come together from north and east. We followed up the northern stream, which in all times has been the true Euphrates and is still called by the name of the lower river, Murad.* Halved though it was now, the Murad appeared still a great river. As we ascended its course the red-brown waters came boiling out of ever-deepening gorges; the last buttresses of the Dersim began to push their roots into it on the east and the foot-hills of Sarichi-chek Dagh to close on the west, until immediately below and above Egin rock-walls rise sheer out of the stream a thousand feet. A road has been blasted and

---

* Here my information differs from all maps that I know. In each and all this stream is written *Kara Su*, a name unknown, so far as I could learn, to the dwellers on its banks. I never heard any other name than Murad from the point of junction right up to Erzinjian, and I asked for the name or heard it casually scores of times. The only designation of the eastern branch mentioned to me was Palu Su.

embanked (and must be re-blasted and re-
embanked every summer) along the water's
edge below the town, but above the point
where the first bridges are no goat could
pass ; and travellers by all roads to Divrik
on the west, or Pingan and Kemakh on the
east, must labour over lofty passes with
here and there a dizzy glimpse of a reach of
Euphrates glimmering two or three thousand feet below. When we had turned
the elbow and set our faces towards Erzinjian we found the hills fall back a little
on both banks, and now, instead of being
prisoned in well-like gorges, we could see
over the nearer heights to the peaks and
glaciers of Dersim.

During the six days' ride from Pingan
to Erzinjian we enjoyed the grandest
of panoramas ; sometimes by our side,
sometimes far below, when we had to
take to the hills, foamed rapid after
rapid of the Great River ; beyond it lay a
strip of green coast, and then the wall
of hills with dark patches in the ravines,
where Armenian villages and gardens

marked the course of some mountain stream, but becoming treeless and naked ere they shot up into a rampart of black rock-needles and white domes, broken by blacker clefts and blue glacier hollows. It is a tremendous mountain mass, this Kurdish stronghold, which has cost the Ottoman Government so much and will cost it more, and the Kurds need assist Nature but very little to close it against all comers—south. north, east or west. Indeed, in all this titanic region of the upper Euphrates Nature has never been modified much by Art. In recent times, indeed, some attempts have been made at road construction ; the maps with which we were supplied showed *chaussées* in the valleys, crossing the river at Keban Maden and bisecting the Dersim ; but in reality between Malatia and Erzerum no wheel has passed as yet. There are short lengths of roadway here and there—for instance, between Arabkir and Keban Maden, or for a dozen miles east of Egin, or in and around Erzinjian ; but except near the latter town, where the roads are kept in order to serve the needs of the Fourth Army Corps, the embankments and cuttings are returning fast to their first state. No ruts cut the macadam, for there are no wheels within a hundred miles; pack animals take the shorter cuts they took of old; and the engineers' abortive creation is left to be seamed by the tremendous rains, cracked by the sun and pared away by the bitter frosts, as winters follow summers.

In ancient days also Nature seems to have been as little assisted; for we failed to find any important Roman works on the right bank of the Great River, which was recognised as the frontier of the Empire, and held against all the East for nearly seven centuries. A long list of frontier guards is recorded in the *Notitia Dignitatum* of the fifth century A.D., under the command of the " most illustrious the Duke of Armenia "—legions at Trebizond, Satala, and Melitene, and a host of auxiliaries, horse and foot, some of whose regimental names reveal that their fore-

fathers had been free men once in Gaul, and
Germany, and Switzerland. Three years
before this I had found a great military
chaussée, roadway, milestones and all, con-
necting Melitene with the interior, and
looked naturally to find another as great
and as prolific in records of its own history on the line of the river itself. But we
found never a milestone, save one only near
Melitene on the road which ran inland to
Sebastea. Here and there, once just above
the meeting of the two forks of Euphrates,
again a few miles north of Aghin, again at
Ashuk, occurred short stretches of paved
road, very rough and ill-laid and little like
Roman work; twice we were guided to ruined
bridges, one over the Angu Chai, which
was without inscription but unmistakably
Roman, when judged by the finely squared
masonry at the spring of its single arch.
The other, over the Kara Budak above
Pingan, remained only in the rubble core
of its abutments, but on the rock above
was a sunken panel recording in bold Latin
lettering that the bridge was built in the

time of the Emperor Decius across this
river Sabrina—an Armenian Severn.   As
to legionary camps little enough remains
of that of the Sixteenth at Samosata ; we
found less even at Melitene, not even a
tile of the famous " Thundering " LEGIO
XII. At Satala fortune was kinder, for
the ground plan of the wall with its square
towers remains on the north and east, and
in the modern hamlet of Sadagh were preserved half-a-dozen tiles of LEGIO XV.
APOLLINARIS : but at Trebizond we could
hear of nothing ; and out of all the inter-
mediate forts saw uncertain traces of only
two—one, utterly ruined, on a high arti-
ficial mound near Korpanik and not far
from the fork, and another, better preserved,
built of polygonal masonry on a low emin-
ence above Pingan, at the meeting of two
small streams a mile away from the river.

The truth must be that there was little
need of elaborate work where Nature had
fixed such a tremendous frontier-line. The
Great River is never fordable below the
junction of its main confluents, while above

that point the Dersim hangs over all the left
bank, as impervious in the time of Xenophon
as now. No large army could come from the
far East through those fearful passes, and
in the days of her strength the Empire
treated mere mountain tribes, whether
Scots, or Armenians, or Carduchi, with a
like easy contempt, drawing a furrow to be
passed at peril, but constructing no scientific defences. In the wild valley of
Euphrates, so little inhabited then and
now, great works, if built, would survive to
be seen still; where such there actually
were (Vespasian's bridge south of Taurus,
is an example), they have hardly changed
in eighteen hundred years. But there was
little need of them; there was no crossing
the eastern frontier in the face of the
weakest garrisoned posts; and the vague
rebellious sentiment of the East could
picture the way of its kings prepared
against Rome only when an angel had
poured out his vial on the great river
Euphrates and the waters thereof been
dried up utterly!

We had found nothing very ancient in Egin. It was probably a mere village or less before the Armenian migration of the eleventh century A.D., and was increased by refugees because of its inaccessible situation. Many " Turks " have settled there now, and the professors of the two creeds balance one another, each holding a flank of a theatre of rocks, which opens on the right bank of the river, and can be entered only by most difficult paths from behind. The streets are slippery ladders, and the roof of one house is a courtyard for the one above; *bazars*, houses, gardens, are huddled together with little fresh air and less light—for the winter sun shines into the bay for only two or three hours— and the great spring at the top of the town which sends three cascades roaring to the river, fills the atmosphere with spray and the damp exhalations of thousands of trees. The air felt cholera-laden : indeed, long afterwards, we learned that the place had been suspect while we were there, and that we ought to have been detained : but an

Englishman is held to be a focus of seditious talk in Armenian towns, and so it came about that, orders from Sivas notwithstanding, we were bidden godspeed by the authorities with much goodwill on the third day, and rode rejoicing over the wooden bridge and up and down wild hills of evil repute for Kurdish robberies, till at evening we reached the river again, bending east at Pingan.

A spectacle had been presented to us in Egin very rare in provincial Turkey—that of a Moslem of high rank become a habitual drunkard. He had been Governor of the place, and, being suspected of a horrible crime of lust and murder, was living under guard in his own house until advices should arrive from Stambul. He insisted, it seems, on being allowed to call upon us, and came at night shuffling between two policemen. We were ignorant of his foul repute but could not mistake his condition, and endured his presence with a very ill grace. Having been in the West, he seemed to have lost all the virtues

of Islam, and to care to talk only of the
vices of Paris, and for two mortal hours
his offensive iteration continued, until the
patience of ourselves and his guards could
endure no more, and he was led back to
his place. Such a specimen of a drunken
official is almost singular in my experience:
I can recall only a renegade Greek, who,
being sent to Gyuksun (Cocusus), consoled
himself in that scene of St. John Chrysos-
tom's exile with unlimited strong waters.
I have suffered many things at the hands of
Ottoman provincial Governors, and more
perhaps than I know; but still I will main-
tain that, taken one with another, their
personalities have been singularly superior
to the system they administer. I have
encountered not a few who were venal,
some who were fanatical and cruel, and
many who were stupid, but very few who
shirked their work and fewer who were
weak. And, all things considered, their
courtesy to a European is conspicuous,
both when he is armed with special permits
and when bearing only the ordinary pass-

port. They might well behave otherwise ;
their interest in keeping the Christian at
arm's length is real enough, for they belong
to a dying race, as they themselves profess
sometimes with pathetic hopelessness ;
every sleeper of every railway means a
Christian advance; every advance means
the retreat of Islam. The map-making,
note-recording visitor from the West is the
herald of a light in which these Turks will
wither one day, and a visitor, knowing that
they know this, can feel no rancour for the
few annoyances, delays, and failures, for
which directly they are responsible.

Divrik, on which we dropped from the
mountain opposite Pingan, was Tephriké,
the final home of " Paulicianism," strange
heresy, blending Eastern dualism with
the Trinity, which first caused Christians
to wage holy war on one another. But
Paulicianism came too late in times too
troublous to leave memorials of itself
on rocks and stones, and we were not
surprised to find nothing in Divrik, except
the lowest courses of the castle walls,

earlier than the magnificent Seljuk mosque
built for Khaikhosru II. Like most Seljuk
buildings, the latter is conspicuous mainly
for its portals, here decorated with deeply-
carved floral ornament, more *flamboyant*
than the work of the Konia Sultans in
Sivas, Karaman, Sultan Khan, or their
own capital. On the side of the north-
eastern portal is carved the twin-headed
eagle, which was a Seljuk emblem before
it reached Europe, and apparently a Cappadocian " Hittite " symbol far earlier still,
since it is displayed on the rocks of Bog-
hazkoï, and the flanks of the human-headed
bulls at Eyuk. The mosque has fallen into
disuse, but is famous still in all Anatolia for
a " magic ball," really a globe of Persian
porcelain suspended in a cupola, and interesting chiefly because in its sanctity survives a last tradition of the mysteries of
Paulicianism.

Once more we found ourselves in an
infected district, but having come into it
without seeing any *cordon* we hoped to go
out equally unchallenged. We chose a

little-frequented path low down near
Euphrates, and were not disappointed ;
perhaps the storm which swamped our
camp on the third night drove the patrols
to shelter, and certainly a second storm,
which gathered all the fourth morning and
broke right over us in the afternoon, made
pursuit, had any been proposed, impossible. We barely succeeded in reaching
the bridge of Kemakh that evening, and
camp and baggage had to stay all night on
the farther bank of a rivulet, now swollen
to a fierce flood, twenty feet from bank to
bank. A sorry night spent in wet clothes
in a miserable room of a miserable *khan*
was followed by a sorry day passed in
desiccation, and enlivened for three of the
party by arrest on the Castle rock. Isolated
and perpendicular on all four sides, this rock
of Kemakh is the strongest natural fortress
I have ever seen, but as it bears no sort of
modern fortification, but only the ruinous
walls and fallen buildings of the Byzantine
Kamacha-Theodosiopolis, our artist sat
down to sketch with an easy conscience.

An Armenian, who had proffered his services as guide, whistled promptly ; with
equal promptitude policemen appeared from
all sides, and, seizing sketch-book and
paint-box, hustled the three Franks down
to their *khan* and set a sentry at the door.
Then, flushed with success, the leader
came down to the Governor only to find
me, all unconscious, in the very act of
showing our special permits from Stambul—
papers, be it observed, of an importance rare
in this remote town. I noticed some con-
fusion and a sudden access of politeness,
but nothing was said of the arrests, and,
taking leave in due course, I returned to
the *khan*, there to find three irate com-
panions. It appeared that the sentry had
vanished a few minutes earlier and the ring
of watching policemen melted away, and,
not being molested again, we swallowed
the insult for fear of being questioned too
closely as to how and where we had passed
the *cordon*, supposed to be closing all roads
from Divrik.

Next morning we repassed the bridge :

beneath it Euphrates was whirling a
tormented scum of sheaves and tree-
trunks and other spoils of its flood, for
which naked peasants were fishing waist-
deep in the red waters. Two easy days'
ride, always along the Euphrates' bank,
with the same stupendous prospect of
snow and black crags beyond the river,
brought us to Erzinjian, lying back from
the river in a triangle of rich plain.
The sound of many bugles smote fami-
liarly on our ears, and the sight of whitewashed barracks and trim alignments
of tents was pleasant to eyes long used to
mud-hovels and pine-log shelters. The
Fourth Army Corps has its station here,
the best-armed and organised in the Ottoman army, and designed to co-operate with
the garrison of Erzerum as a first line of
opposition to a Russian advance. They
certainly looked a formidable force to
reckon with, these well-clad, well-fed
soldiers, who filled every street and all
the *bazar*, and hustled about us asking if
we were Russians ; and they have work

L

enough to do with other foes than the " Moscov," for we barely saved our horses from being requisitioned to help convey a battalion despatched in hot haste to the foot of the mountains, whence serious trouble was reported, the result of the immunity which the Kurds had enjoyed since the massacre described above. And this, it seems, was the outward and visible beginning of the now famous affair of Sassun.

This last lurid page in Armenian history, together with the whole " Armenian Question," inevitably recurrent as an Armenian ague, is *sub judice* as I write and like to remain so.* So far as I understand this vexed matter, the source of the graver trouble is the presence in the heart of Armenia of the defiant Kurdish race, which raids the villages where the flocks are fattest and the women most fair, now cutting an Armenian's throat, now leaguing with him in a war on a hostile tribe, and resisting in common the troops sent up to restore the

* Written early in 1895.

Sultan's peace. Whatever the Kurd does is done for the sake neither of Crescent nor Cross, for he bears neither one emblem nor the other in his heart, but just because he is Ishmael, his hand against every man who has aught to lose.

The Armenian, for all his ineffaceable nationalism, his passion for plotting and his fanatical intolerance, would be a negligeable thorn in the Ottoman side did he stand alone. The Porte knows very well that while Armenian Christians are Gregorian, Catholic, and Protestant, each sect bitterly intolerant of the others, and moreover while commerce and usury are all in Armenian hands, it can divide and rule secure ; but behind the Armenian secret societies (and there are few Armenians who have not committed technical treason by becoming members of such societies at some period of their lives) it sees the Kurd, and behind the Kurd the Russian ; or, looking west, it espies through the ceaseless sporadic propaganda of the agitators Exeter Hall and the Armenian Committees. The Turk begins to repress because we sympathize, and we sympathize the more because he represses, and so the vicious circle revolves. Does he habitually, however, do more than repress ? Does he, as administrator, oppress ? So far we have heard one version only, one party to this suit, with its stories of outrage, and echoing through them a long cry for national independence. The mouth of the accused has been shut hitherto by fatalism, by custom, by that gulf of misunderstanding which is fixed between the Christian and the Moslem.

In my own experience of western Armenia, extending more or less over four years up to 1894, I have seen no signs of a Reign of Terror. I have noted severe repression of national sentiment, amounting to a minor state of siege, but not certain evidence of more than a dozen distinct wanton outrages committed by Moslems on Christians, and no evidence at all that such as really occurred were inspired by a fanatical motive. In Armenia Christian as well as

Moslem lives in a wild mountain land a
wild life with fierce passions unbridled : are
we to expect in the struggle for existence no
acts of cruelty or lust? Life in Christian villages has not shown itself outwardly to me as
being very different from life in the villages
of Islam, nor the trade and property of
Armenians in towns to be less secure than
those of the Moslems. There was till
lately no visible sign, for all the whispered
sedition on the spot or the violent utte-
rances of nationalists in Europe, of that
stagnant abject terror which should go
with the state of things so constantly
credited in Exeter Hall. There was ten-
sion, there was friction, there was a condition of mutual suspicion as to which Armenians have said to me again and again,
"If only the patriots would leave us to
trade and to till!" If the Kurdish Question could be settled by a vigorous Marshal,
and the Porte secured against irresponsible
European support of sedition, I believe
that the Armenians would not have much
more to complain of, like the Athenian

Allies of old, than the fact of subjection—
a fact be it noted of very long standing;
for the Turk rules by right of five hundred
years' possession, and before his day the
Kurd, the Byzantine, the Persian, the
Parthian, the Roman preceded each other
as over-lords of Greater Armenia back to
the misty days of the first Tigranes. The
Turk claims certain rights in this matter—
the right to safeguard his own existence,
the right to smoke out such hornets' nests
as Zeitun, which has annihilated for centuries past the trade of the Eastern Taurus,
the right to remain dominant by all means
not outrageous.

I see no question at issue but this of
outrage. For the rest there is but academic
sympathy with aspiring nationalism or
subject religion, sympathy not over cogent
in the mouths of those who have won and
keep so much of the world as we : Arria
must draw the dagger reeking from her
own breast before she can hand it with any
conviction to Pætus !*

* I wrote these pages before the outbreak of the present

The day on which we left Erzinjian the Great River was seen for the last time in a distant prospect from the lofty pass of Sipikor, whence waters flow this way and that to the Indian Ocean and the Black Sea. Erzinjian was hidden by the foot-hills, but on the farther side of its plain Euphrates glistened as a winding silver thread, and beyond it snows could be seen piled on snows up to a horizon black with storm clouds. Across the line of our road ahead lay long ridges like billows of a broken sea, but less tremendous than those of the region through which we had come, and the head waters of the Lycus ran away from our feet into a green valley of corn-fields. As this pass of Sipikor is the boundary of the maritime province, we were free at last from fear of being turned back and from all risk of quarantine, of which latest

Rebellion; and I let them stand as a record of my own personal experience. It will be time to revise them when we are informed far more certainly than is now the case of the measure of responsibility which lies on the shoulders respectively of the Sultan, the Armenian nationalists, and the wild tribes not really under Ottoman control.

threats had been uttered by the military authorities at Erzinjian ; and with our faces turned to the north we felt a little of the sense of escape which made Xenophon's weary Greeks raise their shout from a point a little further north on this same road. But, nevertheless, we were all more than a little sorry to travel no longer by the side of Euphrates. The ceaseless motion of water exercises a strangely stimulating effect on the imagination in common with other things inanimate but not inert, such as wind and flame. Savages have worshipped them in all ages, and poets been subject to their influence ; and we, although neither savages nor poets, were conscious that for some reason, half understood, no march during the past two months had ever been weary so long as it led us within sight and sound of the Great River.

CHAPTER V.

AN IMPRESSION OF EGYPT.

The land of mystery—The land of stagnation—The land
of mirage—Pharaonic fallacies—Egyptian art—Influences of Nature—The secrets of the grave—
Pharaoh, king of Egypt—The comparative test—The
Circean chain—A day in the Delta—A buried city.

It has been often my fortune to be present at the first introduction of tourists from
Egypt to the Acropolis of Athens. The
party would halt, gaze up the grey rock,
and presently one would speak for the rest,
"Is *that* the Parthenon? How ordinary!"
Now such as these tourists are not necessarily of Philistia ; they have but the minds
of the majority of mankind—emotional, that
is, rather than intellectual, and tending towards superstition. To such cravings as
theirs the Parthenon, which appeals to the
emotions through an intellectual æsthetic
sense only, furnishes but poor food ; for
it is absolutely and altogether intelligible,

the most perfect expression of a race that abhorred the Beyond, conceiving gods that were not Incomprehensibles, and ideals that were all of this world finite. The mind of the majority on the other hand, so far from wishing to follow the Hellene wherever the argument may lead, is drawn powerfully towards the half-known, the unknown, and even the not to be known, craving the stimulus of infinite possibilities behind a half-drawn veil. It looks to be reminded, by finger-posts pointing into darkness, of the existence of a Beyond, but has really no sort of desire that the cloud should lift. Olympus is not Olympus to them, unless seen, as I myself saw it for the first time, detached from earth and sea by low-lying clouds, and lifting, dimly seen through breaking mist-wreaths, its rose-red cone into the heaven itself.

Such superstitious imagining should resort to Egypt. There, where nothing is more than half known, it will find the kindliest soil in the world, stretched along the strange river which geographers have

not stripped yet of all its own mystery, and
penned between illimitable silences. How
little we know of those deserts! We
have not mapped even the Arabian and
Libyan bluffs that are seen all day and
every day from the Nile, and often five
miles behind lies the *terra incognitissima,*
which the Nile peasants of old peopled with
chimæras and griffins, and among whose
nameless terrors their descendants to-day
will not pass a night uncompelled. Does
not the Nilot alone supply enough mystery?
Those who know him best confess most
readily that he eludes their understanding;
he thinks, as it were, in another dimension,
and the stream of his life flows on in the
same bed with civilisation, like oil with
water. Recently a Gallic orator, holding
out promise that a storm should come from
the north and sweep away the British oak,
advised the Nilot to bend like the reed.
Small need to advise him! He would bend
to that storm, if it ever blew, as he has bent
to foreigners since the dawn of time, only to
rise erect again as of old. How many

have come into the valley of the Nile, and
left temples on the mounds and mosques
in the cities, and the work of potters and
goldsmiths, and gravers in the sands, but
no trace on the manner of the *fellah's*
daily life! Each new agency has all to
do over again; each new agency advances
sometimes as far as the last, sometimes
less far, never farther.

Egypt has seen not one Renaissance
but ten—the Renaissance of the Twelfth
Dynasty, when the sculptures of Beni-
Hassan and the gold-work of Dahshur
recalled the standard of the Tomb of
Ti : the Renaissance of the Eighteenth,
labouring up again to an inferior delicacy
in relief sculpture in the eastern halls of
Karnak, at Der el Bahari, in the monuments of Amenhotep III. at Luxor, and of
Seti I. at Abydos : the Renaissance again of
the Saitic Pharaohs, to whose period belong
three-fourths of the more exquisite trifles
sold now in Egypt, and the Renaissance
of the Sebennytics, this last a conscious
effort to throw back. There was a Renais-

sance of the Ptolemies, another of early Christianity, another of the Fatimites, another of Saladin, another of the Mamluks, a last of Mehemet Ali. And the impulse of one and all, almost beyond doubt, came from without Egypt, the Amenemhats and Usertasens being foreigners as truly as the founder of the dynasty that is reigning now. And one and all have left the stream of *fellahin* life flowing on changeless as the Nile. The mud huts now are the huts of the time of King Pepi, the pigeon-houses those on which the temple pylons were modelled ; the plough, the hoe, the *shaduf*, still in use, were known in the fourth millennium before our era. You may see clumsy craft, like those given up last year by the sands of Dahshur after thousands of years, being coopered up to-day in any boat-yard on the Nile. Hour by hour in this world the *fellah* lives like his remotest father : hour by hour in the world to come he hopes to live as his fathers hoped to live, ploughing, sowing, irrigating, reaping to all eternity, gaining no more than necessaries, and asking for no holidays, sure just of life from the unfailing bounty of a celestial Nile. It has been fabled often that a traveller in the Brazils or the South Seas has lighted on survivors of a classic race in some sealed valley. In sober reality a sensation not less strange may be experienced in some parts of Egypt, notably the Central Delta and the Fayûm —a sensation half attractive, half repellent, as among *Struldbrugs*, men overdue to die, corpses walking among the living.

Who shall breathe life into this folk? Who assimilate the *fellah* who has stood aside to let so many civilisations pass him by? It were a task of Sisyphus, if undertaken in earnest! The same melancholy story which results from contact of young and old races all over the world, is only less melancholy in Egypt because, under the natural conditions there, the young race itself seems to age so rapidly, and depart or die. "Stay in Egypt seven years at a stretch, and become an Egyptian," is a saying among Europeans.

The Nile wins you: the changeless sequence of rising and sinking waters wins you, and the sameness of sun and seasons; in the third generation your issue fails, and the last word is once more with the Nilot.

Just because to so great a degree Egypt remains not understood (perhaps not to be understood) by Western minds, it has been named ever since Herodotus Land of Paradox. The Occidental seems to lose all his sense of perspective in the Valley of the Nile, and to see everything looming in a mist of Mirage. The tiniest of countries, it bulks as a colossus; inferior in acreage to Belgium, with a population hardly more numerous than Ireland, it produces the impression of an Empire as one sails painfully up its one highway. The eyes of all Europe converge on a strip of green along the Nile, and we speak habitually of our " mission " to it, as to the immeasurably greater India. Regarded internally, Egypt is but a tenth-rate territory. It

is her debts alone that have given to
Egypt external relations of any importance,
that, which the strength of Mehemet Ali
worked for in vain, having by a strange
irony come about through the weakness
of his grandson. In truth, when other
lands are brought into comparison, nothing
in the Nile valley remains absolutely great
in its kind, saving and except its antiquities and the exploitation thereof for the
tourist! With the monuments began
European interest, and with them it is
safe to prophesy that it will end. When
it has been long forgotten that in a dead
generation Egypt assumed importance in
Bourse speculation, or was a bone of conten-
tion between Powers that have ceased to
contend or ceased to be, the imagination
and the curiosity of the civilised world
will be riveted still on the work of the
Pharaohs.

And we seem to lose sense of proportion as well when we look at ancient
as at modern Egypt. Who, travelling
in the Nile valley, remembers that the

Pharaonic wonders are only the best-preserved and most accessible, not the most marvellous that exist, even as in ancient times there were greater cities than Thebes or even Memphis? That archer-frieze brought from Persepolis to the Louvre takes rank above the best mural decoration that Egypt ever produced, even at Abydos. The Memphite work is not comparable artistically with the Athenian, and Karnak, tried by a standard of magnificent bulk, is outdone by monuments of Rome. The thrill which we feel when we credit the Pharaonic architects with lost arts and more than human ingenuity is born of pure fancy; Karnak, impressive and grandiose in an Egyptian twilight, is an agglomeration of architectural absurdities ; the familiar pylons of the New Empire and the Ptolemies are the most graceless of all possible structures, and those huge figures, which stand stark or sprawl across the courses of their masonry, are rendered barely tolerable by all the sun and all the mirage of the Nile.

I know nothing more saddening than to

M

pass from a study of Greek art to a study
of art so-called in Egypt. Where is
that pursuit of an ideal, that artistic
conscience which inspires every work of
the Hellene ? Look up and down the
Nile valley; look at the structures of
Upper Egypt, the most part well seeming
on the outside, but rubble and rottenness
within, continuously jointed and casually
patched, able to endure only in a land
where frost and rain are not : look at the
gesso laid over walls to cover a multitude
of sins : look at the back or any obscurer
part of a statue, and you will perceive that
the "artist" was influenced as little by any
pride in his work for its own sake, as by
a belief in the omnivision of his gods.
Everywhere one sees temples incomplete,
tombs half decorated, reliefs left in outline,
inscriptions pirated and served up in hideous
half-obliteration. The artists are no better
than artizans, modelling and limning unconsciously century after century gods and
kings and soldiers and slaves, according to
impersonal conventions: twenty generations

serve to produce a modification of but a single detail. The personality of the creator is never once obviously instinct in the creation, and there is hardly a statue in Egypt that suggests for a moment individual inspiration. The most marvellous examples of technique, the Sheikh el Beled for example, or that stupendous Pyramid Builder, who sits in diorite at Ghizeh, are replicas of hackneyed types. The compressed lips of the latter, his square and rigid carriage, his clenched hand might have been taken for an idealisation of Pharaonic majesty, were not the attitude repeated point for point in subject as in king.

Development there was, of course, in Egyptian art, for art, like human character, must move, but not progress to a higher perfection. The movement of the eddying stream is towards the worse from the Old Empire to the days of the Ptolemies, when Greek art came to vivify and stayed to die. The charming, if too precious, delicacy of the work of the Saites had held out promise that when the full flower of Hellenic cul-

M 2

ture was transplanted into Egypt it would
flourish anew in a soil so long prepared :
but what do we find in fact in the Alexan-
drian age ?   A little more idea of symmetry and decorative effect, as in Euergetes'
pylon at Karnak ; a little more reasonable
lightness and abhorrence of brute bulk
at Philæ : in all the sculpture an attempt,
almost grotesque, to make the Egyptian
canon approach nearer the real human
model.   But on the whole the dead weight
of the Pharaonic centuries has crushed the
Greek. He has lost his Hellenic conscience :
he has no heart in his labour ; his uncon-
genial hieroglyphics protrude like worm-
casts from the surface of the sandstone ;
he scamps and he vamps like the veriest
Ramesside. His good points disappear; the
faults of the Pharaonic architects persist ;
the same absurdities of construction, for instance, appear at Edfou as at Der el Bahari ;
the same primitive method of building
in the rough and facing afterwards is seen
on the Roman Arch at Philæ as in the
" Temple of the Sphinx."   What has

been said of the influence of another very old land on new comers may be said of Egypt—there was too much of it, and it was too old! Ptolemaic art is worse every way than Pharaonic—bad relatively and bad absolutely, *corruptio optimi pessima !*

The long stagnation, or long decay, has been laid at the door of the priesthood. How can one symptom be accounted for by another? As well postulate a " conservative instinct " in the Nilot, a third symptom to explain the other two. The common first and final cause is Nature— Nature who has made life so easy and so monotonous in Upper Egypt, where falls not hail nor rain nor any snow, but Nile overflows year by year, certain winds blow at certain seasons, and the sun blazes day by day across an unchanging vault. There are no uncertainties in this life and it knows no contrasts, but seems to follow one course yesterday, to-day, and for ever, without pain and without joy !

There is in Egyptian products the charm

of marvellous technique, that charm which all exquisite handiwork must possess, in the Nile valley as in Japan : there is an environing charm of climate and scene ; but beyond question their most compelling charm is due to the impression made on the imagination by their wonderful preservation. We are promised all the secrets of the grave, and our curiosity is piqued the more that the promise is never fulfilled. For, indeed, despite the curious minuteness of our knowledge, despite those surviving marks of disease on a Thothmes' skin, the loaves and seeds set out for a priest's last meal, the actual boats, the models of menial occupations, the garments intact still, and the implements of husbandry and housewifery, we know hardly more in reality of old Egypt than the bounds of our own ignorance. What can we say of the personality of its mummified kings ? What did they do that was not merely official ? Of what race were two-thirds of them, and why did one dynasty succeed another ? Is the Book of the Dead elaborate artifice of an expert priest-class tenacious of power, or is it popular folk-lore ? Was the Cult of the Dead a spiritual religion, or no more than a studious statement of the common residuum of all religions, that is to say, of a belief in unseen agencies working humanly, in unreasonable retribution ? Did the Pharaonic *fellah* see in Osiris a type of a second life, or just the Sun or the Nile ? Was Egyptian religion in short a polytheism or a simple monotheism of Nature ? No one of these questions can be answered any more surely to-day than yesterday.

So much material exists that it is forgotten often that we lack the one thing needful to History, namely literature. It is only Annals that can be compiled from monuments, and annals even with all circumspection, for nothing in the world lies like autobiographic inscriptions. Contemporary documents carved on stone, whether in Greece, or at Behistûn, or in Egypt, have been accepted often far too literally, the fact being disregarded that the motive to

lie monumentally to posterity is one of the
strongest that actuates human nature.
Has not a sober chronicle been compiled
from the vapouring Ramesside texts,
and the servile hyperbole of Pentaur,
graven on the pylons of Luxor, found its
way into narrative history? Even the
sanest of living Egyptologists is fain to
state that the magnificent fiction of Rameses,
deserted by his captains, routing single-
handed the whole Kheta host, is "founded
on fact!" Surely we cannot accept now
the triumphs which these Pharaohs claim
for every raid on the Bedouin or promenade above the Cataract, yet how often
has Pharaoh been taken at his own
valuation, rather than the truer one of the
Hebrew prophet—"a staff of a broken
reed, on which if a man lean it will go into
his hand and pierce him"! A king who
has raided a little beyond the Arabian
desert becomes Sesostris; the Usertasens,
the Thothmes', and the Rameses', who
establish precarious posts in the Sudan,
levy black mail in Palestine, or conclude

alliances with chiefs of Syrian tribes, are ranked with the great kings of history. Shades of the monarchs of Nineveh and Babylon, who raided the Kheta year by year for a summer diversion! and yet more ye shades of the Emperors of Rome, who held fifty Egypts in the hollow of your hand! Tried by a comparative standard, the only monarchs of the Nile Valley that approach to absolute greatness are Ptolemy Philadelphus I., Saladin, certain of the Mamluks, and Mehemet Ali, for these held as their own what the vainglorious raiders of the Twelfth and Nineteenth Dynasties but touched and left; and I know no prettier irony than that among all those inscriptions of Pharaohs who " smite the Asiatics " on temple walls and temple pylons, there should occur no record of the prowess of the one King of Egypt who really smote Asiatics hip and thigh—Alexander, son of Philip.

Herodotus has to answer for much that he first taught men to dismiss Egypt in a phrase as a Land of Paradox, and all things Egyptian as abnormal. Ordinary standards

and the comparative method are not thought
of to this day as applicable to the Valley
of the Nile.   There alone philologists
could acquiesce all this century in a preposterous doctrine that the ancient language
had no affinity to any other tongue.   The
last great work on the history of Egypt
assumes once more the familiar "thousands
of years" necessary for the growth of art
up to the time of King Snefru, although
when and where else has an art taken more
than a very few hundreds of years to
develop ?   Not in Greece, assuredly, and
not in Italy.   Judged by comparison,
Manetho's first three dynasties would seem
to give time enough and to spare.   And
what a glowing picture of a splendid
civilisation existent in the fourth and
third millennia is drawn from the Tomb
of Ti and the goldwork of Dahshur!
albeit Japan and China have shown that
the utmost delicacy and precision of
handiwork in ivory, gold, and lacquer can
be produced in the night of barbarism, and
certain of the most exquisite monuments

in Cairo date from the bloodiest epoch of
the Mamluks.

It must be for want of comparison also
that Egyptology is spoken of so habitually
by its votaries as if there were no other
archæology, and that discoveries in Egypt
are qualified by absolute superlatives. In
the Nilotic mist Mycenæ, Nineveh, and
Pompeii are forgotten, and Hawara or
Dahshur extolled as the spots where explorers' eyes have seen the most wonderful
resurrections of a bygone age; and yet how
much more marvellous was Schliemann's
great Treasure than even the regal hoard
seen by Brugsch at the bottom of the
shaft of Der el Bahari! To a greater
extent than perhaps any other archæology
the study of ancient Egypt has fallen
within the province of the curious amateur
or the narrow specialist, little acquainted
with any other scholarly study; and only
of late has it seemed to be understood
that some link with the modern world
must be found, or Egypt will remain ever
barren, a Memnon, as Hegel so finely

put it, ever waiting for the day. It is a welcome sign of a better era that so many now raise the question, Is Egyptian civilisation to be found in that road which leads to the light through the two essential ideas of the Hellene, the absolute claim of the community, and the divine image in man, which still inspire all civilisation ?

It must be confessed that little progress has been made as yet in the building of any bridge across the great gulf between Egypt and pre-historic Hellas ; and perhaps it were best to found no great hopes on Mycenæan and Ægean discoveries, but turn, rather, to the later Hellene and to the Jew, the Hellenized Israelite who stands in the gap between the dying order of old Egypt and the nascent Christianity, in an obscure period of transition when all things were passing through the crucible. If it could be shown, indeed, that by way of the Jew or any other, the dogma and forms of the great conquering Faith received a sensible impress from the Egyptian, what new life would be breathed

through all that valley of dry bones where
so many have laboured with ingenuity and
perseverance worthy of a better cause than
Curiosity! The student of humanity, if
he works forward from origins and not
back to them continuously from himself, is
apt sadly to stray; his long study is stale
and unprofitable; and the self that he
consecrates to a lifelong research is left a
stepping stone to nothing.

So seem things Egyptian here in the
cold and critical North, where the mind
springs back, astonished to have been en-
chained so long by the spirit of the Nile.
But all seems otherwise within sight of
the holy stream, and no Ulysses ever has
resisted altogether the Circean charm of
Egypt. It is a charm indescribable, a charm
of landscape largely, instinct in the sun-
soaked stillness of gleaming river, of vast
green levels, of fantastic rocks and of
wind-blown sands. Let the sun be
darkened ever so little, and the charm is
gone from the grey waters and the dingy

flats. But there is another charm, even more
seductive, in that condition of life-in-death
and death-in-life which pervades the land
and its people. If anyone has not experienced this let him stand on the
brink of a high desert bluff and look
behind and before, at the immensity
of the death and the narrowness of
the strip of life, and reflect what would
happen to the last if some convulsion of
Nature diverted the Nile for a single
week. Or let him pass from contempla-
tion of a sphinx of the Middle Empire
or a Der el Bahari mummy to a village of
the eastern Delta, and see the almond-
eyed water-carriers stalk along, impassive
ghosts of three thousand years. Or best
let him turn off beaten tracks and visit on
the extreme east or west of Lower Egypt
one of the dusty *tells* which break the long
salt flats. It shall be such a brilliant April
day as intervenes between scirocco and
scirocco, when sky and earth are overfull
of light, and a shimmering mirage confuses
the ring of the horizon. Along the new

dyke-road little dust-clouds move above
knots of Libyan Bedouins, riding withdrawn in the folds of their cloaks
towards the Lesser Fair of Tanta.
Here a buffalo wallows, to be distin-
guished in the brown ditch by the little
cloud of flies buzzing over his motion-
less mask. There, a few boys sprawl
recumbent under a rare roadside tamarisk,
and a naked *fellah* hoes his patch of half-
washed land. Now take off from the road
across the canal and keep along a narrow
lumpy ridge, turning and doubling among
irrigation channels as only an Arab path
will do, until you have skirted the last
village, a study in the faintly contrasted
browns of mud walls, mud roofs, stagnant
pools, and naked babes. And now you
are in full marshland, riding over a crisp,
caked surface, threading among treacherous
hollows, out of which whispering rushes
stand shoulder high. Woe if you must cross
such a spongy belt! The sharp hoofs of a
donkey penetrate like pins, a camel slips all
ways at once, and your horse haply will seek

relief from flies and sun by rolling self and
rider in the ooze. Now and again sandy
ridges stand up, seeming mountainous in so
great a flat, advance posts of the not distant
desert; but the dominant feature in the
landscape is a great hog-backed *Tell* which
has slowly been assuming solidity as the
mirage receded behind it. A last hour
goes by, the camels groan through the rim
of the slough, and emerge on to a sandy
tract strewn with countless potsherds, red
and black, and with glittering bits of
iridescent glass.

The *Tell* is not so high as it loomed
two hours ago, but far more extensive
than you had thought, a miniature mountain, indeed, cut into ridge and valley by
the Delta rains. Labour up its soft slope
and look around: a buried city is at your
feet. What had showed from afar as two
peaks of the Mound are really groups
of houses, their roofs gone, and the rooms
filled up with wind-blown sand and dust of
their own unbaked bricks. The scouring
north breeze keeps the tops of the walls

always visible, and you may see as on a map the whole plan of the town, with its narrow, interlacing streets. Between the peaks lies a deep depression enclosed by a ruined rampart open at one end : the soft dust of its surface is mixed with chips of red and black granite and marble, and at one end two broken granite shafts and a corner of an architrave break the level. There is no chessboard of brick chambers here, for this is the site of the great Temple of the city, buried twenty feet deep at least beneath the ruin washed down from its great enclosure wall. Only at the eastern end stand up remains of a huge pylon, whose salt-rotted bricks crumble to dust as you lift them. Except for a little plundering for lime, and digging for nitrous earth by the sparse peasantry, the site is probably virgin : the city under the sand was abandoned to the salts when irrigation failed and the marsh began to spread, and for hundreds of years it has been dead in a dead land, preserving like one of its own mummies the frame and shell of what once

N

it had been.   A Levantine or a European
some day may set there his factory or
dwelling-house and bring back life : but
it will be a life new altogether, the life
of a new race in a new era, no revival of
that hoary spawn of Nile whose fading
force no elixir can restore.

CHAPTER VI.

CYPRUS.

THERE is a legend, received by the
monks of Chrysaorgiatissa, that their holy
picture of the Virgin by St. Luke was
borne by the waves to the beach of Paphos;
and in honour of the Maid of Bethlehem
the peasants of Kuklia anointed lately, and
probably still anoint each year, the great
corner stones of the ruined Temple of
the Paphian Goddess. As Aphrodite was
supplicated once with cryptic rites, so is
Mary entreated still by Moslems as well
as Christians, with incantations and pass-
ings through perforated stones to re-
move the curse of barrenness from Cy-

priote women, or increase the man-
hood of Cypriote men.   The cult of
Woman, lapsing into voluptuousness, and
rising again to chivalry, has been always
dominant in the island, inspiring a con-
tinuous romance, which begins with the
Idalian and the Paphian and closes with
Berengaria and Catherine Cornaro.

For myself, Cyprus has never lost altogether its charm of romance, not only
because there is shed about it a certain
féerie du premier voyage, but because so
much exists really in the island to carry
one back to the nursery world of dragons
and princesses and knights errant.   The
mere passer by Larnaca or Limasol sees
none of these haunts of old romance, but
only dull patches of cultivation aslant
behind dingy towns, or disafforested salt
hills and the mean mass of Mount Troodos.
One must visit Nicosia, lying at the island's
heart in a star-shaped *enceinte* of Venetian
walls ; or better Famagusta, inhabited now
by some few grave Turks, who keep school
within the Crusaders' bastions, and send
from the minaret of a French Gothic

Photo by R. Elsev Smith.

CATHEDRAL OF FAMAGUSTA FROM THE N.E.

[To face p. 180.

Cathedral their call to prayer echoing
through grass-grown aisles and across a
wilderness of broken heraldry down to the
desolate quays ; or best, to the castles on
the northern hills, St. Hilarion, Buffavento,
and Kantára, which the Greeks call Heka-
tospitia, the " Hundred Halls." Choose
the last in spring. You stand on the
spine of a serrated limestone chain which,
falling gradually on your right, runs out
between two turquoise seas, and on your left
bends northwards in a vast blue crescent,
jagged like a crown. Two thousand feet
below, to the north, lies a narrow strip
of forest, and across a misty sea, crawling into innumerable tiny bays, you may
descry the wild Taurus of Karamania, rising
step by step to the snows. And commanding
all this matchless prospect stands Kantára
itself on a pillar of rock, its broken walls clinging to the lip of the precipice, and its great
gate opening on a labyrinth of ruin, crowned
by a little windy chapel. No painter has
conceived a fairy castle more fantastic, no
poet set his enchanted palace in a solitude

more profound.   Richard found it there,
as he found farther west Buffavento and
St. Hilarion, which he was sore put
to it to capture, for their walls were
so high that his missiles fell back on
his own men-at-arms.   But for how many
centuries before his time Kantára had
looked out over the two seas of the Car-
pass, and who built it and why, no one had
been able to say.

Beside these cathedrals and castles or
that exquisite cloister at Bellapais, the
remains of older periods make but a
poor show in Cyprus.   The sites of
its royal cities, Salamis, New Paphos,
Curium, Lapethus, Soli, Amathus, choked
with heaps of coarse Roman rubbish,
offer hardly one stone on another;
and the excavated ground plan of the
Temple of the Paphian Aphrodite is more
interesting than impressive.   But of the
smaller products of industrial art the island
has proved a veritable mine, and the interest of Cyprian archæology consists mainly
in these.   The most part are very similar

in type, of a singular local character, a rude
unglazed pottery, for instance, wrought
into fantastic shapes of animals and sus-
pensory vessels, or a glazed ware, ill turned
and ill baked, ornamented with primitive
incised undulations and hatchings. These
vessels are extracted from the older tombs
by hundreds ; and from the newer, a more
graceful but less characteristic ware and
abundance of local glass : while both in
the tombs and here and there on desolate
hilltops or by streams, where have stood
little shrines of local gods, innumerable
statues and statuettes are found, fashioned
out of the soft native stone, very unmistake-
able and showing a kind of belated archa-
ism in their rigid pose and uneasy smiles,
which is really the result of rustic unhandi-
ness. The Phœnician relics found in the
island, other than the handiwork of Tyrian
hirelings, are few, and pertain mostly to a
kingdom set up in Citium in late times ;
and their scarcity serves to remind us that,
whatever Phœnician repute Cyprus may
have acquired from a doubtful identification

with *Chittim*, or from Herodotus' story of
the bringing of the Paphian Goddess from
Ascalon, the cardinal facts of the island's
early history are these ;—that her primitive
people spoke Greek, called their goddess
by a Greek name, ἡ Fάνασσα, the Queen,
and adopted, to express their speech, a
syllabary so little adapted to Greek, that it is
difficult to believe that they can have had
an early knowledge of the convenient
Phœnician alphabet. All over the island
rocks and statue-bases and gems and pottery are found engraved with the characters
of that strange syllabary and these add a
peculiar attraction to Cyprian exploration.

Probably, however, there is not much
more to find now that is new ; for the
island has been mined for treasure ever
since Christianity prevailed sufficiently to
destroy fear of the old gods and of the
dead. When digging at Paphos, we found
that a labyrinth of passages had been cut
from tomb to tomb by early robbers, working underground for weeks or months, but
plundering in such haste or such obscurity

that their leavings were well worth raking over again : and recent excavators for the British Museum say that they seldom (if ever) opened a virgin tomb. If so much has remained nevertheless, both for ourselves and for them, and to form also that wonderful Cesnola collection at New York, what must not the wealth of the Cyprian sepulchres once have been! Had other resurrectionists not been before him, Cyprus would be now a digger's paradise; there the thorns, incident to excavation in the Levant, are present least of all For there are such thorns, *experto crede !* in a trade which is often credited with being the most labourless form of excitement in the world! The Levant is far from being one vast "lucky-tub," into which whoso putteth his hand will draw out a prize. Schliemann, the most fortunate, Petrie the most systematic of excavators, have drawn in their time the blankest of blanks ; for unless some accident of landslip or erosion or, better, the patient grubbing of native seekers give a clue to

what lies beneath a *tell* or in a hill-side,
you must begin always, more or less, in
the dark, according as your experience
is small or large, and topographical *data*
precise or vague, and must put often to the
account of design that which chance directs.
And sometimes others, that come after,
find where you failed. Moreover, even
where success is sure, long days must pass
without a discovery to break the monotony
of watching a mound slowly diminishing
or a trench being cut painfully into packed
earth among encumbering stones; in
Egypt, a blinding, stinging dust rises from
centuries of foul refuse, disturbed by the
workmen, and chokes nostrils, eyes, and
throat; or, as at Salamis in Cyprus, the
sand, which ever slips down into your
trenches, is alive with sandflies and fleas.
The sun scorches and the rain beats, and
you must endure them both, for you can
never safely leave your workmen to dig
alone; and, for all your vigilance, they
will mar and break, and withal they will
steal.

In Cyprus, where tombs are wet, the workmen, turning over with their knives the mud or that unpleasant soapy earth which results from human decomposition, would wipe their blades every now and again on the soft walls ; and at night creep back to the scene of the day's labour and away again with a gem or a ring that had remained in the lump scraped off. The Egyptian sees a *scarab* shine in the falling dust and, covering it with his foot, works it up between his toes, until the moment when it can be transferred safely to his cavernous cheeks; and in that receptacle it will lie all day, causing no inconvenience, for the *fellah* is accustomed so to carry coins, like the peasants of all hot countries, who must strip to work.*
Search the thief and he will swallow the scarab or gem without thinking twice. Nothing will secure you against robbery altogether, where a market for stolen objects

* Hence, no doubt, the ancient Greek practice of putting money in the mouth of the dead.

exists, not the sternest measure dealt out to delinquents, nor even Mr. Petrie's plan of paying market price for all small finds ; for the Oriental usually will not sell in the first market that offers, be the price what it may. The method of payment also has two grave drawbacks, one, that it leads to the "salting" of a site with imported or spurious finds, the other, that in a land where fine distinctions as to *meum* and *tuum* are not understood, it gives the workmen reason to regard what they find as their own : nor can the method be applied at all where, as at Luxor, small antiques, good, bad and forged, are on sale at a preposterous premium.

Cyprus, however, while it has an obvious advantage in being administered by enlightened officials, has this count, too, in its favour, that mistrust intervenes less there than anywhere between an explorer and his men. I have reason to believe that we were robbed hardly at all at Paphos, in 1888, simply because there is

little or no market for antiquities anywhere
in Cyprus, least of all in the wild west,
and our workmen were so many unsophis-
ticated children. None of our personal
belongings, leave them about as we might,
were ever stolen; and the gold pin, now
one of the glories of the jewel room in the
British Museum, was found by a man
working alone out of sight of his fellows
or ourselves in the last inch of soil above
the rock. When there is no need to search
the persons of the men, or lay traps, or
play policeman, digging becomes a mighty
agreeable pursuit and profitable in many
ways. You may not learn much archæology
—indeed I doubt if digging ever trains
a young scholar to do much else than
dig—but you will learn much about your
men, their customs, their superstitions,
their folk-lore, their racial character ; you
are become their medical and their legal ad-
viser; they will consult you as to the barrenness of their wives and the advisability of
divorcing the same ; they will apply your
drugs to wholly new uses, and ensure their

efficacy with supplementary rites of sorcery :
they will introduce you to their dream-
world, which is an equal half of their life,
and to impossible folk-tales untainted by
euhemerism.   And above all, if by fair
dealing you have gained their confidence,
they will speak with much candour on
the subject of their pastors and masters.
We dealt as fairly as we knew how to deal
at Paphos and never closed our door, and
this way and that came to know something
of the Paphiti in particular and of the
Cypriotes in general.

The Paphito is simply the raw material
of the old Hellenic stock.   Latent in him
are those qualities which give to his more
advanced brothers of Rhodes, Symi, or
Leros, so peculiar a position in Egypt,
and so distinct a character in Athens and
Europe.   He represents, in fact, the pure
" island " element in the new Hellene, that
ancient strain in the latter's blood which
brings certain marked qualities, that can
be recognised fuller and fresher in antiquity, to be combined now in Greece

[*To face p.* 190.

DIGGING IN THE APHRODITE TEMPLE AT PAPHOS, 1888

Photo by R. Elsey Smith

with the characteristics of younger and ruder races. No one, who knows it, can regret that this remnant of the ancient Hellenic stock possesses but little vitality. Those great and noble qualities, which the modern Greek has displayed so conspicuously this century past, belong to him, to my thinking, in spite, not because, of his possessing a little old Hellenic blood. The stock, that was *græculus* even in the Augustan age, has been passing down the road of racial decay these two thousand years. It was precocious, it lived fast, and tired soon, and now, because it is not quite wholly extinct, the new Hellene has to combat in himself a decadent influence, certain ignobler traits being owed by a strange irony to the blood of the same race whose tradition has done so much to ennoble him. Everyone who has been in the Levant knows the decadent island type— and many do the new Hellene the injustice of supposing that there is no other—the *græculus* who lends money in every market of Egypt, makes and sells strong waters

to Moslems in most cities of Western
Asia, and calmly awaited the coming of
the Mahdi at Khartum, sure, sooner or
later, to spoil the spoiler. He is shapely and
shrunken, with extremities over small, and
teeth close set and level as if filed, and he
has a very genius for trifles. Much lies
beyond, but nothing beneath him, and, like
the Jew, lending sixpences in the day of
small things, he is content to turn over and
over the mere interest on his capital, when
trading on a worldwide scale. In him
the old Hellene's great virtues survive
in little, independence decayed to self-
assertion, self-restraint to servility, keen
intelligence become a superficial sharpness,
and courage fidgetty nervousness. Not
that his decadent descendant is a coward,
though many have dubbed him so who
knew him little, Thackeray, for example,
with his libellous "armed to the teeth but
afraid to fight!" No! he will fight still, not
as an Irishman, for the love of it, nor with
the unimaginative phlegm of a Scot, but as
a quivering thing that flies at a big man's

throat. I have taken two Cypriotes into inland Asia Minor. The first, a Christian, lost the rest of the party for three hours in a Circassian district, and, when found, was speechless and ashen grey, seeming ten years older than in the morning. The other, a Moslem, but none the less a Hellene in blood, talked of Kurds all day and dreamed of them all night, broke out in cold sweat at sight of an armed shepherd, and was white with impotent terror in the ferryboats on Euphrates. But whenever general dangers threatened to become concrete, both one and the other stood his ground.

As to the Hellene of the Roman age, so to his last descendant in Cyprus the petty war of party politics, municipal if not national, is singularly congenial. Hardly emancipated from sheer rusticity, he picks up all the tricks of the trade, learns the use of parliamentary weapons and the abuse of forms. Nothing strikes a stranger, who may chance to assist at a meeting of the Cypriote Legislative Council, more than the demeanour of the Greek members ; they

o

have a programme, an organisation behind it and a mastery of some of the methods of free debate which might excite the envy of an Irish Nationalist.

Fortunately for the Paphito, cultured Europe has not made him her spoiled child, nor has emulation of the West induced him to try to disguise the fact that he is by nature an Oriental. His language is an orderly product of his history, untouched by patriotic purists, and he has forgotten altogether the savour of the fruit of the Tree of Knowledge. But he has the same quick intelligence and ready adaptability as his more civilised brother, the same fidelity to his kin, the same domestic virtues. And his shortcomings are those of low development, not inherent vice, of one who will steal a sheep and shoot the shepherd, but scorn to commit petty larceny, one who is a very rude child of nature, happy in the blankest squalor, and untaught equally in religious enmity or reverence for priests. His god is a private god, jealous of trivial observances and un-

reasonable in revenge, ever present in the
fields, but to be sought in the church only
on a few feast days,—the common god, in
short, of all the half civilised, Christian
or pagan. Like generations of his fathers
he lives on in his flea-ridden mud hovel,
and tills a stony patch of arid land, being
always in debt for his taxes, and often in
prison for his violence, unashamed, unam-
bitious, and wholly unconscious that others
can be ambitious or ashamed.

There are some odd corners in our
Empire, and Cyprus is certainly one of the
oddest, in a sense a superfluous island,
taken no one knows why, to be given to no
one knows whom. Now it hangs suspended
in the atmosphere of British administration
between the Sultan, to whom it belongs,
and the Hellenic kingdom, to which it
would fain be assigned. The Cypriotes
are still Ottoman subjects, and if they
migrate to another part of the dominions
of their suzerain, are not entitled to a
British passport or British protection,

while, being under British administration, they have no Ottoman passports. In return for this British administration they pay debts of the Porte, not contracted on their behalf, the British Treasury kindly supplying the annual deficit caused by this payment in the island Budget. The whole arrangement is desperately illogical and patently absurd, a consequence of a vague design taken up suddenly and as suddenly dropped, a flagrant example, indeed, of the evils of party government applied to Imperial affairs. We put our hand to the plough in 1878 and have looked back ever since; having done enough to detach the island from one Empire, we have done next to nothing to attach it to another. At present it oscillates " betwixt being and not being," and is no sort of use to anybody. It should be borne in mind that internally Cyprus has no particular sources of wealth or power; for Nature has not been over bountiful to the island, as we count bounty now; it is harbourless, stricken by droughts, and locust ridden, if continual and costly

war be not waged on the pests ; it has
no navigable rivers, hardly any forests,
and no wealth of minerals worth the
working. Its corn, one year taken with
another, scarcely suffices for home consump-
tion ; tobacco has never been planted, since
the island, being still Ottoman in name, is
subject to the monopoly of the Turkish
Régie ; silk culture makes little way where
there is so little water for the mulberry trees ;
grapes and charub-beans are good crops
but command a most precarious market.
The only real importance that Cyprus has
ever possessed has been owed to its
position as a half-way house in the Levant.
In ancient times it was a *caravanserai*,
wherein East met West to prosecute in
common a congenial nature-worship, with
rites less bestial than in Syria, more sensual
than in Greece. A thousand years later
it became a refuge and rallying point for
the relics of the Crusaders, and, all other
ports being closed, the place of gathering
for Christian traders concerned with the
alienated East. But always its prosperity

came from without and it looked seawards, profiting by an accident of position to take toll of the products of other lands as they were exchanged against each other in its convenient harbour of Famagusta.

Except, therefore, for the possible account to which its geographical position relative to Egypt, the Canal, and Syria could be turned, there was no possible ground for our taking over its administration in 1878. No bitter cry against Turkish misrule had ever gone up from this particular island : and the older Cypriote Greeks admit now that they were not oppressed, having been, indeed, in some ways favoured specially by the Porte. Nowhere in the Levant used there to be less religious antipathy, and even as late as 1888 I recall that the funds of a church in the wild district of Papho were devoted by the priest to saving a Moslem from distraint for taxes, and subsequently punctually repaid. If Cyprus was to profit by our presence, or we were to profit by her possession, we were bound to put her into relation with the world outside. As a fortified naval station she might have commanded the coasts of Egypt, Syria, and Anatolia ; with a harbour for large vessels, she would have absorbed much of the deposit trade that now goes to the dangerous road of Beyrout ; and with a regular mail service to and from Egypt her mountains must have become the great sanatorium, not only for soldiers but for civilians concerned in the administration of the Nile valley. But what has happened in fact ? After nearly twenty years of our occupation, Cyprus does not possess (so far as I know) a single gun for coast defence or a harbour capable of floating anything larger than a fishing smack ; Limasol and Larnaca have only open roadsteads, too shallow for ocean-going steamers to approach within half a mile of the beach, too little sheltered during the prevalence of certain winds for any ship at all. There is no regular mail service ; and, now that the half battalion of garrison has been withdrawn, Troodos will hardly be used even as a military sanatorium.

We have given to Cyprus no expansion, no part in any Imperial or commercial scheme. Our capital and enterprise avoid the island for want of a guarantee that it will be administered by us always ; the energy and goodwill of our administrators is clogged hopelessly by that ruinous and iniquitous mortgage with which we allowed the " new jewel " to be encumbered when we set it in our Imperial crown. We can hardly complain, therefore, if the Christians, disappointed from the firstand disheartened still more by the small result of their deputation to the Colonial Office in 1889, hold meetings on most high days to pass resolutions in favour of annexation to Greece ; and indeed, as a matter of fact, we do not complain at all, having some conscience, and being wont also, above all other nations, to preserve a leonine composure under foreign criticism and comment. But the leonine attitude out of season has a perilous resemblance to criminal indifference. Cyprus is left like a little triangular heap of dust in an unregarded corner, and the spectacle is neither edifying nor reassuring. For this island is, to all intents, a member of our Empire, and a member of an Empire, as of a body, become inert, is dangerous to the rest in proportion as itself decays. One of two courses must be taken in such a case; the member may be nourished into taking its part again in the organism; or it must be cut away.

Cut it away, then—but into whose hands is it to pass? By the law of nations Cyprus is the right of the Sultan, by the law of nationality of the King of the Hellenes. The historical claim of the latter might afford a theme for endless academic dispute, but his national claim cannot be questioned; for, however little Cyprus entered in past ages into the Hellenic communion, it is, without doubt, Hellenic now, become identical with the new Greek nation by community of speech and creed, of tradition and hope. Unhappily, however, so satisfactory a solution of the problem would be little practicable

in the present state of Hellenic finance ;
and we should confer a most questionable
boon on the Cypriote, were we to hand
him over to undergo the compulsory military service and tremendous taxation of a
kingdom, which, having for the present no
effective fleet, could not protect him.　The
case of Corfu, so often quoted, is in no way
parallel, for when made over by our Com-
missioner that island passed unencumbered
and endowed with every advantage of
nature and art to a community whose
territory lay distant not a day's sail, and
whose resources had not then been called
in question.

There is, however, another country
which could put forward a certain claim to
Cyprus, a claim based on history and
geography, in accepting which we should
do no administrative injustice.　Egypt has
been overlord of Cyprus longer and more
often than any other power.　Alexandria
lies now less than a day's steaming from
Limasol.　In our own military arrange-
ments we have found it possible to include

Cyprus in the Egyptian command, and there would hardly be more practical difficulty in subordinating its administration civil and military to the Khedive. Since the Sultan's suzerainty would persist, removed but by one degree, no fresh violence would be offered to the sensitive tradition of the Caliphate. Egypt is better able than Greece to supplement the Cypriote exchequer, and far more likely to so increase the trade and finance of Cyprus by opening a new market and establishing a summer colony on its hills, that presently the grant-in-aid might be extinguished altogether. To the Moslem Cypriote such a transference would be grateful ; and the Christians too would gain by becoming Egyptian subjects rather than Ottoman, even were there not, as there perhaps is likely long to be, a European protecting power in Cairo. The lot of the Greek under the Capitulations in Egypt is singularly desirable from his own point of view, a fact evinced by a steady immigration of Hellenes into the Delta : and the

Christians of Cyprus, being so largely pre-
ponderant, might reasonably be guaranteed
at the time of transference such a semi-
independent status as has been obtained
for Samos.

By some such redistribution of the cards
we might redress honourably our imperial
blunder of 1878, confessed now by ministers
themselves in the House of Commons. Up
to the present we have some reason to claim
that we have fulfilled, perhaps as thoroughly
as could be expected in reason, the obligations which devolved upon us. In spite of
fetters, financial and diplomatic, our mark
has been set on the island, a mark perhaps
deeper and more lasting than any other
race would have impressed, manacled
as we. And even as Corfu still seems
neither Greek nor Italian, but in a sense
Northern, so Cyprus will long retain, perhaps never lose, a sort of Western air—
the air which Nicosia wears now, as one
approaches from Larnaca, something of the
aspect of a mediæval ruin set in a modern
park. The promenade round the Venetian

bastions, the fosse swept and garnished, the cleanly kept streets within, the well levelled roads without, the wire fences enclosing tracts of scrub, and the white rails and gates of trim gardens, are European exotics among the minarets and the palms.

And not only on the surface is the presence of a Western power evident, but in the confidence of men who travel alone and unarmed, neither cower before nor run from an official, speak their minds freely, and appeal as a matter of course to the law. The Cypriote has learned that officials can be incorruptible, and public servants zealous, and what is meant by a law that does not respect persons and alters not. Even the Moslems, who distrusted us so much at first, have gained political confidence, and begun to build themselves upper chambers, and invite a second blade of grass to grow where once it was not worth while to raise one for the tax-gatherer. But with the sense of safety the desire of progress has been born and Cyprus can never relapse to the condition of Syria or Anatolia. More than that, she can never be content to remain always as now. She has been set by us in the path of development, and, either we must take her further progress wholly and frankly into our own hands, or we must put it into others as capable and as honest. If we do neither of these things, but hold on to the island merely for want of courage to let go, we shall end by obliterating all gratitude for such benefit as in twenty years our administrators have laboured loyally to confer.

THE END.

BRADBURY, AGNEW, & CO. LD., PRINTERS, WHITEFRIARS.

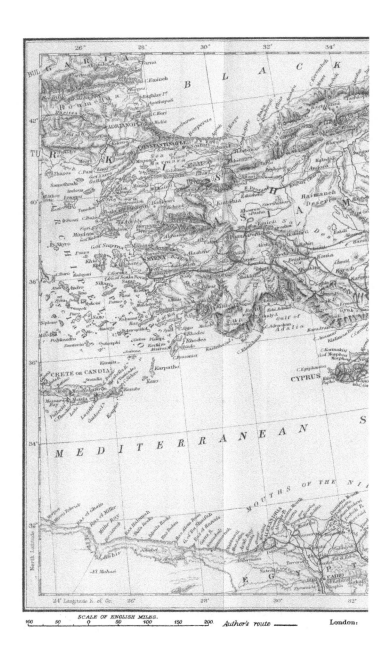

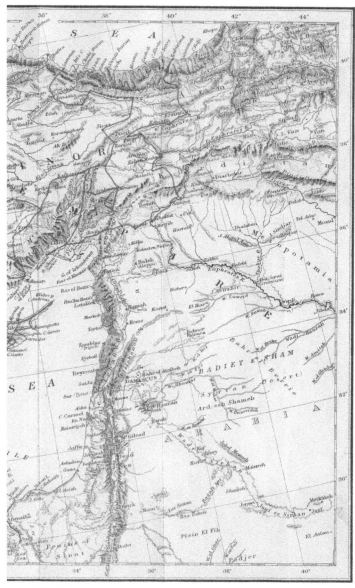

John Murray.

For EU product safety concerns, contact us at Calle de José Abascal, 56–1°,
28003 Madrid, Spain or eugpsr@cambridge.org.

www.ingramcontent.com/pod-product-compliance
Ingram Content Group UK Ltd.
Pitfield, Milton Keynes, MK11 3LW, UK
UKHW010339140625
459647UK00010B/706